"Margaret Randall's new collection of essays is a profound and passionate rumination on the significance of creativity and language. In a time when the word "meaning" is often scoffed at, Randall is not afraid to say words matter: how they are written, spoken, read, and acted upon. Randall's views are strongly held and her essays are often provocative, inciting the reader to dialogue, all the while demanding critical thinking and reading on their part. The essays in *Last Words* are essential reading for anyone who wants to understand some of the most important questions of our times through the experience of a woman who has devoted her life to both writing and living her words."

– Susan Sherman, author of *America's Child: A Woman's Journey Through the Radical Sixties*

"For the better part of her publishing life, six decades or so, the gifts of Margaret Randall's boundless and courageous curiosity, her genius for friendship, love of language, and fearless candor have strengthened and inspired thousands of readers, many of them her close friends. To read *Last Words* is not to witness someone's experience of the end, but to revel once again in the ongoing adventure of Randall's imagination, which welcomes our own explorations of the world revealed to us, she writes, by the 'capacity to think beyond the confines of lived experience,' as we extend ourselves 'outward in unlimited, unexpected, and magical ways.'"

– V. B. Price, author of *Lucretius and the Logic of Venus*

"Once again, Margaret Randall reminds us of what our values should be. Her essays on fascism and religion are must-reads for anyone who cares about our world—and America at this time in our history. There are also joyous ruminations here—her life amongst the Abstract Expressionists in New York City—her love of language—her peaceful life with her wife Barbara in New Mexico. Randall reveals her continuing vitality in *Last Words.* Luckily for us, I'm certain these won't really be her last."

– Greg Smith, painter

"In nine short, contemplative essays, Margaret Randall reflects on what has mattered most to her in her long life of social engagement, political activism, and above all poetic creativity. From her ode to discipline, to her review of the 'fascist arsenal,' to her embrace of 'the ongoing wonder of being,' you can read this collection as a meditation, but also as a handbook."

– Mary Louise Pratt, author of *Planetary Longings*

"An embrace to you, and others with you, taking on the advantage to the world with a new book by Margaret Randall. We all know she crosses rivers."

– Bob Arnold, author of *Faraway Like the Deer's Eye*

Last Words

Selected books by Margaret Randall

Nonfiction

I Never Left Home: Poet, Feminist, Revolutionary

Thinking about Thinking

Haydée Santamaría, Cuban Revolutionary: She Lived by Transgression

Che on My Mind

To Change the World: My Years in Cuba

Gathering Rage: The Failure of Twentieth Century Revolutions to Develop a Feminist Agenda

Poetry

Time's Language II: Selected Poems, 2019–2023

Time's Language: Selected Poems, 1959–2018

Home

Vertigo of Risk

Stormclouds Like Unkept Promises

Oral History

When I Look into the Mirror and See You: Women, Terror & Resistance

Sandino's Daughters Revisited

Christians in the Nicaraguan Revolution

Sandino's Daughters

Spirit of the People: Vietnamese Women Two Years from the Geneva Accords

Last **Margaret**
Randall Words

essays

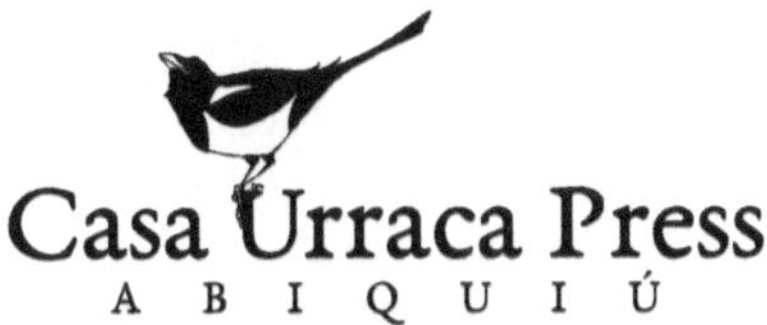

Cover artwork by Barbara Byers.
Author photo by Magdalena Lily McCarson.
Set in Nobel and Marion.

27 26 25 24 1 2 3 4 5 6 7

First edition

ISBN 978-1-956375-34-3

CASA URRACA PRESS

an imprint of Casa Urraca, Ltd.
PO Box 1119
Abiquiú, New Mexico 87510
casaurracapress.com

This book is for
my beautiful family
as it extends
from one generation
to the next.

Contents

In the dark times
Will there be singing?
There will be singing.
Of the dark times.

– Bertolt Brecht*

*. "Motto." *The Collected Poems of Bertolt Brecht*, trans. David Constantine and Tom Kuhn. W. W. Norton & Co., 2019. Originally from the 1938 collection *Svendborger Gedichte*, written by Brecht while in exile in the Danish countryside.

What Matters

LOOKING BACK ON MY LIFE, I realize that I always tried to be close to people who broke the rules, especially artists and writers whose work shattered barriers, showing me that I could do the same.

My first such mentor was the painter Elaine de Kooning.[1] She was a woman and an artist unencumbered by the gendered restrictions of the day. I owe her much of the strength I've been able to develop as a woman in a patriarchal world. Nancy Macdonald, with whom I worked at Spanish Refugee Aid in the 1950s, was a similarly generous teacher.[2] Around the same time, I sent a few of my incipient poems to

1. Elaine de Kooning (1918–1989) was an abstract and figurative painter who also wrote brilliantly about other artists.

2. Nancy Macdonald (1910–1996) was a social activist and founder of Spanish Refugee Aid, an organization dedicated to caring for the Republican refugees left stranded in France and North Africa at the end of the Spanish Civil War.

William Carlos Williams, the elderly doctor and groundbreaking poet who lived across the Hudson in New Jersey, and he invited me to visit, an encounter that gently but powerfully set me on a generative path through language, eventually enabling me to find my own voice.

Most of the poets and visual artists I knew in New York in those years were a good deal older than me: Elaine and Willem de Kooning, Pat Passlof and Milton Resnick, Robert Mallary, Larry Rivers, Alfred Leslie, Jerome Rothenberg, Joel Oppenheimer, Frank O'Hara.[3] Despite the age difference, which in most cases translated as well into a difference in artistic maturity, they received me on what felt like equal terms. Established poets invited me to read with them. Several well-known artists illustrated my first two poetry collections. Their acceptance and support were tremendous boons to my own self-confidence.

When Liberation Theology charged Latin American revolutionary fervor in the 1980s, I sought out an Italian priest philosopher named Giulio Girardi who studied atheism at the Vatican; he was one of a very few Catholic priests who openly opposed the canonization of John Paul II. Girardi modeled that what really mattered in the struggle for justice was justice itself, not blind belief. Because I am a longtime atheist, he provided the perfect bridge to help me understand the importance of what was going on in that new theological movement.

Laurette Séjourné, Ramón Martínez Grandal, Ruth Hubbard, George Wald, Adrienne Rich, Gerda Lerner, Mark Behr, and my wife Barbara Byers: my list of mentors

3. Willem de Kooning (1904–1997) was born in Holland. He was one of the most successful of the Abstract Expressionist painters. Pat Passlof (1928–2011), Milton Resnick (1917–2004), Robert Mallary (1917–1997), Larry Rivers (1923–2002), and Alfred Leslie (1927–2023) were visual artists. Jerome Rothenberg (1931–2024), Joel Oppenheimer (1930–1988), and Frank O'Hara (1926–1966) were US American poets.

is rich in identities, influences, and creative sustenance, and all gave me invaluable gifts of imagination and critical thought. I feel immensely privileged to have had the guidance of women and men who defied established assumptions. They showed me that in breaking new ground what truly matters isn't only desirable but possible.[4]

The more experiences of difference we explore, the better equipped we are to ask generative questions and become familiar with legitimate alternatives. And the more we can know what matters—and what matters to us. But conditioned as we are to "make nice" rather than stand up for our beliefs, it can be a challenge to conserve our integrity while maintaining our friendships.

Consider the following. Someone says or does something that makes you uncomfortable or that you find deeply offensive. Unable to entirely hide your feelings, an involuntary gesture or facial expression betrays you. The person in question asks what's wrong. Rather than speak honestly or deal with raw emotion, you say: "It doesn't matter." You forfeit speaking you own truth to absolve the other person of discomfort or blame. What you are telling them is that their feelings are more important than yours. Our society tends

4. Laurette Séjourné (1911–2003) was a Franco-Mexican anthropologist and author whose work shed light on Mesoamerican culture. Ramón Martínez Grandal (1950–2017) was the exceptional Cuban photographer who taught me that art. Ruth Hubbard (1924–2016) was an Austrian American feminist biologist. George Wald (1906–1997), who studied pigmentation in the eye, won the 1967 Nobel Prize in Medicine. Adrienne Rich (1929–2012) was a US American poet and essayist whose innovative work broke barriers for women as well as for language. Gerda Lerner (1920–2013) was an Austrian American feminist historian. Mark Behr (1963–2015) was a South African novelist who started out spying on the ANC and became a double agent for that organization. Barbara Byers (1952), my wife of thirty-eight years, is a visual artist. Living with her has taught me a great deal about art and about the world.

to favor the so-called harmless lie over honest exchange. We possess rich language but avoid using it if it shatters a conventional or comfortable surface. As a result, we are unaccustomed to sharing what we and others deem important, believe in, or care about. You say it doesn't matter, but it does.

In high school during the 1950s, a particularly suffocating decade for women and girls, I wanted more than anything to be popular. I dreamed of being a cheerleader, maybe even my senior year's homecoming queen, dreams so far beyond my reality that all they brought were anxiety and a constant sense of failure. I longed to date the captain of my school's football team. My idols were Hollywood icons Elizabeth Taylor and Doris Day. Earlier, as a young teenager in successive attempts at making friends and gaining some measure of belonging, I'd joined the Episcopal church (a last brief foray into the dark realm of religion), twirled a baton (clumsily), and exercised my chest muscles in a vain attempt at cleavage: all efforts to emulate the quietly seductive all-American girl-next-door image so prized by my culture and time. Such were the absurd personae that mattered to the girl I was back then.

It's true that I also experienced increasingly frequent moments of more authentic desire: to travel the world, know peoples different from myself, become a writer, satisfy my curiosity about so many mysteries, and communicate my own burgeoning ideas with originality and power. Unusual for the time, my parents encouraged these tendencies. They had followed some unusual dreams themselves, rejecting their own parents' stultifying lifestyles and moving the family west when I was ten, and later taking us on adventurous summer trips on freighter ships.

My childhood home had books and art. My father spent the entire summer between my first and second years in primary school helping me learn to read, a skill I hadn't been able to master along with the other children in my class. Dad was a frustrated musician who had suffered societal limitations in his own childhood. His father was a stern Prussian businessman unable to communicate meaningfully with his three sons, and the family was Jewish at a time when Jews were still subject to entrance quotas at the best US universities. The move west enabled him to establish his independence and find his place in life as a public-school music teacher.

My mother, a tragically dissatisfied woman who grew up in an extremely dysfunctional family and searched endlessly for an outlet through which she might express her creativity, applauded the little stories I wrote and much later celebrated my first self-published collections of poetry. Until her death, she helped proofread my books, attended my poetry readings, and delighted in my successes. Looking back, I have come to understand that she longed to see her own ambitions realized in me, her oldest daughter. As a young woman, she had quit high school to attend New York's Art Students League and made somewhat derivative sculpture. Later she devoted herself to translation. Both my parents were proud of my artistic tendencies. They supported and encouraged me insofar as they were able. Still, because our country doesn't really value creative pursuits, aspiring to be a writer always felt to the young woman I was back then like bucking society. And my family and friends, prey to the same constraints that governed us all, were mostly unable to understand the seriousness of my passion.

As a girl child in the 1940s and '50s, I wasn't even expected to study math or science at the public high school I attended. Girls weren't routinely given that opportunity until 1957, when the Soviets launched Sputnik and the US was desperate to catch up with its archrivals. We took something called home economics, meant to prepare us to be wives and mothers, while the boys took shop, where they were taught to build things.

I was groomed to marry a man who would support me and with whom I would have an appropriate number of socially adapted children. My brother, the only male among three siblings, was encouraged to attend the university of his choice. My sister and I were expected to content ourselves with our hometown state university, an institution which—at least back then—didn't offer much in the way of an intellectual or creative challenge. After all, it was assumed that we'd inevitably leave school to marry. I attended for a couple of semesters, then quit out of boredom and a gnawing restlessness. From then on, I dedicated myself to acquiring an education on my own, often in unorthodox ways.

The society in which I grew up saw the world through a strictly binary lens. We were taught that we lived in the best nation on earth and naturally inhabited an important degree of superiority. White male children were raised to be entitled in every way their class and culture permitted. White females were raised to help boys and men succeed, and to make them feel good about themselves if they didn't. Despite my parents' close relationship with a lesbian aunt and her partner, a woman-loving option was never considered a possibility for me. As a result, and because I couldn't imagine an alternative, I embarked on a long series of heterosexual relationships.

Most of those relationships were fleeting; others produced unhappy marriages. I tried hard to fulfill what society expected of me, but an impatient unease upended any chance for genuine connection. My stubborn sense of self refused the gendered double standard. I couldn't accept the inequality others saw as "just the way things are" and refused to forgive the male transgressions implicit in the excuse “men will be men.” It wasn't surprising that my heterosexual marriages and other unions all ended in failure. Neither was it unusual that their collapses always felt like they were my fault, the result of some personal inadequacy. Somehow, I couldn't live up to the expectations the last half of the twentieth century demanded of me and women like me. It wasn't until 1969, when I discovered feminism, that I began to understand that those failures weren't mine but were rooted in patriarchy's gender inequality.

Feminism changed the course of my life. It mattered, powerfully.

Of course, the change was neither immediate nor unidirectional. I would continue to struggle through a series of unsuccessful relationships with men, having children with three of them. I worked against the social tide even as I taught my son to live by feminist values and encouraged my three daughters to insist upon them.

It wasn't until I was in my late forties and back in the United States that I could acknowledge my lesbian identity and, after a few false starts, establish the relationship I've delighted in now for close to forty years. What matters most in our union is mutual respect and trust, a life built around shared politics and art, a gentleness that defies the brutality around us. We have banished competition, jealousy, and pettiness from the life we share. Over the years, we've discovered that we matter to one another in ways that simply ignore society's hypocritical norms.

Another important discovery was my early need to be part of the struggle for social justice. As far back as I can remember, I sensed there was something wrong with the world around me. I felt the injustices long before I could understand what produced them or name those responsible. I read voraciously, took part in endless discussions with my peers, and joined the political protests of the day. Again, I went down several roads, choosing different ideas and organizations with which to align myself. As a white, middle-class product of mainstream America, my quest for justice wasn't motivated by my own poverty or hardship. I wasn't able, back then, to understand the ways in which predatory capitalism, or being a woman or queer, determined many of the injustices in my life.

Here the issue of choice is worth examining. "Better to be safe than sorry" was an oft-repeated adage when I was young. I had to learn to distinguish between rash decisions and those that might present real opportunities. Additionally, the girls and women of my generation grew up with many fewer choices than our male counterparts, and we had to fight harder—often facing ridicule or shame—to explore them.

What choices we did have were deceptively presented. We were led to believe that if we took the more interesting or ambitious route we would pay with loneliness and grief. Because I was fortunate early on to find mentors who were brave enough to model risk, that quality not only looked like a viable choice to me, it became a touchstone throughout my life. When faced with choosing between safety and risk, I've frequently chosen the latter. It might entail danger but the reward is worth it. These choices haven't always been easy, but they have taken me to places I wanted to go.

Of course, when choosing risk, I also have to consider its consequences. Making risky decisions requires that I be willing to live with the choices I make, bear up under their hardships, occasionally pay a high price. I have to decide what really matters and what doesn't, not only for myself but for my family and the larger world. This requirement has sharpened my understanding of what really does matter.

It took me many years to learn that my passion for justice was most likely born when my maternal grandfather sexually abused me before I had the capacity to defend myself. Ironically, he was a "man of God"; other family members referred to him as a saint.[5] Those who suffer such assault often become abusers themselves in later life or else go in the opposite direction, committing themselves to change for themselves and others. I had dissociated from the incest, erasing it from my memory only to retrieve it in therapy in middle age, long after my grandfather's death. By then, my knowledge of power dynamics, schooled in feminist theory and practice, helped me to see my life without the blinders society is so good at imposing over our eyes.

So, from an early age, for this reason and others, justice mattered to me. At first my search for it was largely personal: how to avoid situations that would limit me, how to free myself from parental and other controls, how to travel where the action was and take meaningful part in that action, how to surround myself with models who showed me what a life that prioritized creativity could be. Gradually this passion became deeper and more specific even while in some ways broader and more inclusive. I have been privileged to know and work alongside people with original ideas who gave their all to building a better world. Imperfect and eventually doomed as it was, our David and Goliath struggle mattered.

I traveled to Spain, then to New York City, Mexico, Cuba, and still later to Nicaragua. None of these stays were brief; they lasted years: a quarter century in all. I went knowing where I was going, drawn by authentic social change, and learned a great deal about how it works in different historical and cultural contexts. I integrated myself into local efforts, experimenting with trial and error on the ground. The courage it took to inhabit those spaces and times, early

5. Early on a traveling jewelry salesman, and always an inveterate womanizer, my grandfather converted to Christian Science at midlife, becoming a Christian Science practitioner and the First Reader at the Second Church of Christ Scientist in New York City.

on as a single mother of a small child and then with four children in tow, was important. It mattered. It also mattered that I didn't simply end up in those countries or struggles. It wasn't about finding myself in the right place at the right time. I sought out those struggles intentionally and with conviction.

Through it all, an element that mattered and continues to matter is my identity as a writer, particularly as a poet. It became the core of who I am, my truest voice. Inhabiting an art form that allows us to express our changing consciousness and grow is vital to a creative life. Art is a world unto itself. Those of us fortunate enough to live in that world cultivate tools that prove useful for the duration. We exercise a probing sensibility and reach. I cannot imagine an existence outside those parameters. Art matters in ways impossible to describe to those who are unmoved by it or aren't engaged in making it themselves.

My children, grandchildren, and great-grandchildren also matter in ways that are difficult to define. I don't believe every woman must choose to be a mother, or that genuine relationships with children who are not one's own can't also be profound. But there is something particular about giving birth and seeing one's offspring grow and develop into whole human beings. To recognize in them features that you possess and others that surprise you. To watch them give birth to families of their own and observe the qualities and talents you've instilled repeat themselves in successive generations. The sense that what is passed on matters.

I have lived at a time when the strong belief that we could change the world has gradually been supplanted by a realization of devastating failure. Despite the promising social experiments of the latter half of the twentieth century, we couldn't bring about the change we envisioned after all. The social revolutions that took place in underdeveloped countries claimed socialism as their goal but proved to be no more advanced than the bourgeoise revolutions that had already been won in France and elsewhere so many years before. Greed and violence replaced a strong sense of community and joyous sacrifice. Trotsky's concept of the need for permanent revolution is relevant here.[6] Processes won at tremendous cost and to which so many gave their all were also decimated by a human tendency toward prioritizing one's own wellbeing, succumbing to the temptation of corruption, and losing sight of the common goal. Capitalism, in all its seductive decadence, won the day and continues to evolve in ways that are more and more disastrous to greater numbers of people. Relationships based on competition took the place of those rooted in equality and solidarity.

For a while, members of my own and successive generations experienced an almost immobilizing sense of defeat and shame. We have bequeathed our children and grandchildren a broken world, and I cannot imagine the despair felt by young people today as they must grapple with the problems we couldn't solve. In this context, it's taken me a while to realize that the ideals for which we fought remain important. They matter.

Time can be a devious companion. Humans experience its passage as unidirectional, measuring our lives and their events according to its arbitrary construction. It may take a redefinition and re-accommodation of our relationship to time for us to fully understand that our struggles haven't been in vain, that the essence of the present moment contains deeply meaningful accomplishment even when it doesn't seem to by conventional standards. We couldn't achieve what we set out to do, but our ideas and actions

6. Trotsky posited that a revolution cannot really be "over" because contradictions will continue to develop, and that it is necessary to perpetually resolve emergent contradictions in favor of the revolutionary program while resisting the risk of sliding back into reaction.

stand as powerful evidence of what is surely necessary and may one day be possible. Those ideas and actions continue to matter.

Literature, music, and the visual arts not only open doors but can walk us through those doors, enriching our imaginations and introducing us to new ideas and feelings. Exploring the best in the artistic expression of every age is one of the most profound ways of experiencing what has mattered to people throughout time. From images painted on the walls of a cave forty thousand years ago to a sophisticated symphonic performance or a poem shouted out on the street by a young person today: all bear witness to our innermost passions and yearnings.

And there are other things that matter, gestures that too often fade into a sort of invisible fabric that undergirds the larger aspects of living. One of these is empathy, the capacity to see and hear others, to give them room and acknowledge their importance. Such gestures may seem unimportant in the grand scheme of things. But small acts of kindness and compassion go a long way towards mending a broken society. At times, they may be all we have.

These days we are surrounded by those who desperately need our kindness. The unprotected are everywhere, walking our streets, homeless and hopeless. Often, they experience mental illness, evicted from treatment programs by society's current tendency to scrap the safety nets that were once available to such people. A few dollars may make the difference between hunger and a hot meal. We might think before excusing a decision not to give with the preconceived notion that, if we do, the recipient will only spend it on drink. One of the few rights such folks have left is deciding how to spend a handout.

It matters that we realize we can't be the judges of how they spend what is surplus to us. In the unusual heat of a scorching summer, a bottle of water can be lifesaving.

In winter cold, a coat or blanket may make the difference between life and death. Revisiting our attitudes towards society's most marginalized members matters not only because offering such small kindnesses is the right thing to do but because a sudden economic downturn, a perfect storm of other unexpected events, or the slightest shift in luck may be all that lies between having enough and needing such help ourselves.

Just as important as paying attention to the needs of individuals, it matters that we develop an awareness of the needs and limitations of our planet. As we've used and abused unrenewable resources for centuries, humans have created a crisis in the sustainability of all life, causing untold extinctions and promising an unsustainable future. An intense struggle is taking place today between those urging immediate action and those intent upon ignoring the signs. Periodic climate summits produce non-binding documents, urging but not requiring that nations reduce their use of fossil fuels. This vital problem just doesn't seem to matter to those who are literally putting an end to life as we know it. The same old rules of engagement—exaggerated economic expansion, greed, despair, indifference—keep us from the courage of commitment needed to reverse course before it's too late.

And what of war, a scourge that has become all but constant in the world? How can we make peace matter, really matter, not to the conscious few but to enough of humanity so that we may finally put an end to the indiscriminate killing and maiming that distorts today's relationships between people over land, resources, cultures, and belief systems?

As I write this, more than forty-five armed conflicts are taking place across the globe—in Ukraine, Afghanistan, Cyprus, Egypt, Iraq, Palestine, Israel, Libya, Morocco, Syria, Turkey, Yemen, and Western Sahara, to name only some of the most flagrant. These wars respond to geopolitics, extreme nationalism, greed, religious friction, and other differences that with another mindset might be decided peacefully. Sometimes war is sparked by an egregious lie, such as the US's false claim in 2003 that Iraq possessed weapons of mass destruction. Once engaged in battle, we claimed we had to finish the job. The idea that war can ever lead to peace is a proven fallacy. For those who aren't suffering it in the flesh, war has become a nameless, faceless, distant event, whose horror seems fictitious because it has nothing to do with us. For those in the line of fire it is a different story.

Take Israel's ongoing assault on Gaza as one example. A few statistics—which will surely have increased by the time you read this—should suffice. Since October 7, 2023, when Hamas attacked Israel and caused 1,200 deaths,[7] Israel's genocidal retaliation has claimed more than 32,200 lives in Gaza, 13,750 of them children. It has wounded more than 74,500 people. It has put three-fourths of Gaza's hospitals out of commission, along with many government ministries and more than one hundred heritage sites. It has destroyed sixty percent of the homes in Gaza. Israeli forces have murdered 123 journalists, many along with their entire families. In comparison, during the twenty years of the US American war in Vietnam, sixty-three journalists died. As of March 2024, this genocidal war has displaced eighty-five percent of Gaza's population.[8] The purpose of what is only the latest in decades of Israeli attack on Palestine seems to

7. Israel's own estimate. Hamas, voted into power in Palestine, is a terrorist organization. Its attack on Israel responded to decades of Israeli occupation of Palestinian territory, ever-expanding Jewish settlements on the West Bank, and other policies aimed at controlling and belittling Arab natives.

8. These statistics regarding Israel's assault on the Palestinian people are from the daily report issued by the Palestinian embassy in Uruguay.

be to wipe the nation from the map, pushing any remaining inhabitants of Gaza and Cisjordan out into the Sinai desert; it constitutes nothing less than ethnic cleansing: a crime against humanity. Prime Minister Benjamin Netanyahu has indicated that, when the assault ends, he will empty out a strip of land almost half as wide as Gaza itself as a safety zone to protect Israel.

By any measure, these numbers should matter to the world. They represent genocide in every sense of that term. At the International Court in the Hague, South Africa accused Israel of genocide, and successive UN General Assembly votes to condemn the attack have ended with an overwhelming majority of countries voting to condemn—a vote long vetoed by the United States, which finally abstained rather than veto in March 2024, allowing the resolution to pass. But Israel has managed to present itself as victim and aggressor simultaneously. And a carefully constructed campaign over many years has succeeded in equating anti-Zionism with anti-Semitism, making it extremely difficult for anyone to criticize Israel's policies without being called an anti-Semite.

Decades of Zionist propaganda, successfully equating anti-Zionism with anti-Semitism, has profoundly affected worldwide public opinion. Here in the United States, university presidents have lost their jobs, professors and students have been silenced, artists have had exhibitions canceled, and actors have forfeited important roles, all because they have dared protest the genocide. Even when such people lament the losses on both sides, it isn't enough. This is a dramatic instance of what matters being sacrificed to deliberately orchestrated censorship.

It's as if a moral condemnation is all we can muster, in a time when morality no longer moves those who hold political power. At this point, US governmental support is the only thing shoring up Israel's genocidal action.

I say every life matters, Israeli and Palestinian alike.

Turnaround is extremely difficult in war, but it is possible. In terms of climate change and other problems, we have viable options. How can we prove that walking back the damage matters? That it matters more than just about anything else?

It often seems as if we've reached a tipping point, past which the opportunity to right our wrongs is rapidly becoming impossible. The enormity of our challenges may lead us to decide none of it matters, that there's nothing any of us can do—individually or collectively—to shift direction. That it's already too late. The thing is: what matters always matters. Even when the chances of success seem slim to nonexistent, it matters that we try.

And trying may be the only thing left that matters now.

What Is Art?

THIS QUESTION HAS TWO PARTS: what constitutes and defines a work of art as such, and what role it plays in our lives. To the second I would say that from art's earliest manifestations—images inscribed on the walls of caves millennia ago, objects remaining from cultures long gone—it has expressed the meaning and creativity of every age, projected a human imaginary, and allowed us to feel emotions more intensely and deeply than we can express in mundane communication. Masterful art displays the originality and power of the person who created it. It can also change our perception of reality and show us who we are in the world.

The first part of the question is more difficult. At distinct points throughout history, our understanding of what art is has changed dramatically. Much art stresses the elegant, beautiful, or purely decorative; it is often meant to project harmony and delight or represent social status within the acceptable framework of a given culture and time. In recent decades, we see art that has become more daring, art that insists itself into ever-bolder transgressive renditions designed to challenge viewers rather than simply gratify them.

I began to think about the ideas embodied in this essay after viewing and listening to my friend Roberto Tejada's 2023 Wyeth Lecture in American Art.[1] The artists he features, work he shows, and ideas he explores move me profoundly. Some of his examples also trigger painful memories and challenge my understanding of what art is. This text is meant to be in conversation with him.

Since my earliest memory, art has been an important part of my life. As a child, I was taken to museums, a practice I have continued wherever I've happened to be in the world. I've contemplated a broad range of paintings, sculptures, photographic images, and examples of other artistic genres from many different cultures and times. Early on I was most impressed by the mystery and glitter of such examples as Egyptian funerary finery and old European painters with their imposing masterpieces. At the age of six or seven, a larger-than-life statue of The Winged Victory of Samothrace gave me my first conscious sense of female strength and agency. Later, my contact with the pre-Columbian cultures of the Americas led me to a deep appreciation of their art and architecture, which then extended itself to an interest in the expressions of other ancient cultures. I've been

1. Roberto Tejada (1964) is a US American poet and cultural critic current holding the Hugh Roy and Lillie Cranz Cullen Distinguished Professorship at the University of Houston, where he teaches in the departments of English, Creative Writing, and Art History. Since 2003, The Wyeth Foundation, named for the artist Andrew Wyeth, has provided financial support to the National Gallery of Art in Washington, D.C., by sponsoring scholarly gatherings in the form of an annual lecture or symposium (in alternating years) related to important topics in American art.

excited by public art, most prominently murals—from the Mexican mural movement to that of the San Francisco Bay Area and the flowering of mural art in so many cities today.[2] I also became enamored of photography, even becoming a professional photographer myself for several decades. Living among the Abstract Expressionists in 1950s New York City put me in contact with their work. Over a lifetime of intimate contact with art I've naturally developed my own preferences and tastes; many other artistic expressions throughout the world continue to speak to me in powerful ways. My book called *Artists in My Life* is a tribute to some of the art that has enriched me.[3]

My wife, Barbara Byers, is a visual artist. She has worked in acrylics, photography, collage, prints, digital illustration, and the creation of artist books, among other mediums. We have collaborated on many projects, Barbara contributing the visual art and I the written text, but have never considered either of our work to be an illustration of the other's. Rather, they move in tandem—each with its own presence—much like our relationship. Our separate practices are integral to our life together. We have moved twice and, to the surprise of family and friends, hung the art we own by many different artists even before arranging our furniture in a new space.

When the painter Elaine de Kooning and I first met in New Mexico in the 1950s, I introduced her to the bullfights in nearby Ciudad Juárez, Mexico, accompanying her to those Sunday morning rituals and watching her make the sketches that would become her famous bull series. Later,

2. The Mexican mural movement began in the 1920s in the wake of the Mexican revolution. Its main proponents were Diego Rivera (1886–1957), José Clemente Orozco (1883–1949), and David Alfaro Siqueiros (1896–1974).

3. *Artists in My Life*. New Village Press, 2022.

in New York, she took me with her to sporting events at Madison Square Garden, where she made rapid drawings of the athletes in powerful motion. Those experiences taught me how a skilled artist can take quick notes and later turn them into more studied canvases. As an incipient poet, I translated this to my own writing practice, keeping a little book in which I could jot down ideas and phrases which I might access later in more finished works.

Art has always had a visceral effect on me. I experienced my first orgasm in my early twenties standing before a Mark Rothko painting at New York's Museum of Modern Art.[4] Masks created by artists from many different cultures have drawn me into their worlds of altered identities. The art and architecture of different cultures has sent me on veritable pilgrimages: to the world of the Maya and Inca, in search of Monet's paintings in French museums, and to visit every one of Mary Elizabeth Jane Colter's innovative buildings on the south rim of Grand Canyon.[5]

My understanding of art is inclusive rather than exclusive. For example, I have never understood the elitist definitions given to separate *art* and *craft*; they are indistinguishable to me. I find that work moves me dependent only on its quality, on how brilliantly it projects the artist's imagination, uses the materials it employs, successfully combines form and content, and challenges me to look in new ways. Similarly, I reject the term "primitive art," which implies

4. Rothko was an abstract painter who was born in Daugavpils, Latvia, in 1903 and died in New York in 1970. He is known for large canvases with two or more fuzzy-edged areas in different colors.

5. Colter (1869–1958) was an architect and designer at a time when there were few women in the field. She worked for many years for the Fred Harvey Company and designed many of its railway hotels as trains opened the western US to tourism. Her buildings on the south rim of Grand Canyon are particularly noteworthy.

that the artist is inferior because less formally schooled. Whether artists trained at a prestigious art school, learned by apprenticing, or are completely self-taught, what they produce speaks to me (or not) irrespective of limiting labels.

The question remains, though: What is art? The Oxford Dictionary defines it as: "The expression or application of human creative skill and imagination, typically in a visual form such as painting or sculpture, producing works to be appreciated primarily for their beauty or emotional power." Like most dictionary definitions, it is concise and quite narrow.

Plato developed the idea of art as "mimesis," which in Greek means *copying* or *imitation*, while Aristotle believed that art is a form of expression with the potential to be appreciated for its beauty and creativity. He said that art is a human construct and should not be seen as a replication of nature. Instead, he argued, it is an imitation of a higher ideal, which can be found in beauty, truth, and morality. Most early definitions saw art as aristocratic or divinely inspired.

The German philosopher Friedrich Nietzsche also approached art in religious terms: "Art is essentially the affirmation, the blessing, and the deification of existence," he wrote. But the Catholic monk and author Thomas Merton offered a more secular and evocative definition. He said: "Art enables us to find ourselves and lose ourselves at the same time." Georg Wilhelm Friedrich Hegel, another German philosopher, thought art expresses the spirit of a culture as well as that of individual artists and the general human spirit.

More contemporary thinkers and writers have continued to speak of the subject in different ways. The US American poet Robert Frost wrote: "To me the thing that art does for life is to clean it—strip it to form." Martin Heidegger observed that art either manifests, articulates, or reconfigures the style of a culture from within that culture's world. The Irish poet and playwright Oscar Wilde believed that "art is the most intense mode of individualism that the world has known," while the French novelist, art theorist, and minister of cultural affairs Andre Malraux wrote that "art is a revolt, a protest against extinction." The African American writer and civil rights activist James Baldwin said: "The precise role of the artist is to illuminate that darkness ... to make the world a more human dwelling place." The Bulgarian-born, US American-based essayist Maria Popova wrote that "Art is ... the power to transcend our own self-interest, our solipsistic zoom-in lens on life, and relate to the world and each other with more integrity, more curiosity, more wholeheartedness." Speaking in Marxist terms, art can be understood as a part of the superstructure or as part of the material base. In other words, it can be understood as ideology or as technology.

The cultural critic Lucy Lippard responded to my asking her what art is by replying: "I've never been into pinning it down. Whatever people say it is, I'm in, though liking or even agreeing is another story."[6] Poets and writers seem to be particularly interested in speaking about their work, although for us over-explanation is a danger. At public readings I've too often had to listen to poets explain a poem away before they even begin to read it.

Visual artists, although often reluctant to explain or dilute what they do by articulating it in words, have been more abstract in their musings while at the same time probing more deeply: the Spanish artist Pablo Picasso famously remarked, "Art is a lie that makes us realize the truth."

6. Lippard (1937) is a US American writer, art historian and critic, activist, and curator. She was among the first writers to argue for the dematerialization at work in conceptual art and was an early champion of feminist art.

To me, the more interesting definitions are not those that reduce or confine art's meaning but those that recognize its varied identities and potential, pointing to new ways of thinking about its capacity to astonish and point us in new directions.

In Roberto Tejada's Wyeth lecture, he focuses on several contemporary Latinx visual artists, whose work contests the colonialist images that the dominant culture repeats, mirroring the classist and racist history that has subjugated the artists' cultures for so long. They are concerned with neocolonialism, migration, displacement, racism, violence, death, and other issues, as well as with ongoing restrictions to their identity, integrity, and power. Some of these artists are queer, and their work rejects the binary assumptions imposed by heterosexist law and stigmatizing social norms.

Such transgressive art exists in every community that has suffered oppression and repression because of class, race, gender, sexual identity, religious dogma, memory erasure, or any other reason. Nineteenth-century ledger drawings by Native Americans of the Great Plains chronicle white colonial genocide. Africans kidnapped and brought to the United States as slaves produced many different sorts of art that reflected the terror of the Middle Passage, life under slavery, and human resilience in the face of horrific conditions. Japanese Americans sent to US internment camps during World War II also made art in difficult circumstances; the sculptor Isamu Noguchi spent time in one of those camps.[7] The Holocaust, Cambodian genocide, Latin America's "dirty wars" of the 1970s and 1980s: all have produced a legacy of deeply moving art.

The artists who made and continue to make this work too often receive pushback, censorship, and even punish-

7. Noguchi (1904–1988) was an artist and landscape architect who voluntarily spent time at Poston Camp in 1942.

ment from the official artworld and its gatekeepers or from others who consider themselves guardians of morality. In 2001, Santa Fe's Museum of New Mexico hung a painting by Los Angeles artist Alma López in which an image of the Virgin of Guadalupe appeared clad in a midriff-baring two-piece bikini covered with flowers, reminiscent of the traditional Virgin of Guadalupe's cloak on which flowers are said to have miraculously appeared.[8] The artist claimed her portrayal was of the Virgin "as a modern woman, a strong woman, like us." Then-Santa Fe Archbishop Michael Sheehan protested the inclusion of the painting on the grounds that it was offensive to the Catholic faith. To the museum's credit they did not take it down.

Cuban artist Angel Delgado made an even more extreme statement in 1990 when, as part of a show entitled *The Sculptured Object* at the Centro de Desarrollo de los Artes Visuales in Havana, he squatted in a roomful of people and defecated on a copy of the Communist Party newspaper, *Granma.*[9] He called his performance *Hope Is the Last Thing That We're Losing.* He was imprisoned for six months as a result. Although he had studied at his country's Academia Alejandro and Instituto Superior de Arte and had been making art and showing it for a while, this act launched him into the public eye inside and outside Cuba. And these are just two of many examples of artists whose transgressive work speaks to social and political issues in powerful ways.

Tejada's lecture focuses largely on Latinx artists who live along the US/Mexico border. It begins with multimedia artist

8. López (1966) is a Mexican-born Queer Chicana artist whose work often portrays historical and cultural Mexican figures, such as the Virgin of Guadalupe and La Llorona, filtered through a radical Chicana feminist lesbian lens.

9. In 2005, Delgado (1965) left Cuba and now lives in Long Beach, California.

Luis Gispert and his radically altered cheerleader images, what the artist calls a "mutable pop icon long fetishized in US culture and media but in configurations that defy the laws of gravity."[10] Defying gravity, a scientific reality we tend to take for granted, is in and of itself transgressive.

The Puerto Rico-based duo Allora & Calzadilla, Houston-based Celia Álvarez Muñoz, and other artists appear, each with their own way of relating to the brutality with which the US mainstream tries to erase their traditions, disrespect their identities, take away their agency, and destroy their lives. Perhaps because of my years in Mexico and my passion for her ancient cultures, the work of Celia Álvarez Muñoz made a particular impact on me. Álvarez Muñoz produced *Petrocoatl, Aztec God del Fin del Mundo* (1992), a polychrome wall drawing of a fictional Aztec deity. Petrocoatl is loosely configured to resemble depictions in the Codex Borbonicus, a document that features images of Mexican gods in full regalia, among them Xipe Totec, Huitzilopochtli, and Tlaloc. Tejada explains that: "Petrocoatl might at first look like one of those gods, but on closer inspection you see that his attributes include a green- and red-feathered ritual cape and headdress as well as a shield with a front-facing skull and an apron with a black oil drop referencing the petroleum industry. His head and face are covered with a protective gas mask, equipped with a respirator, as though the deity were prepared or preparing for chemical, nuclear, or biological disaster." I have long been familiar with the renderings of pre-Columbian figures in the codices, on pottery, and on the walls of the Mesoamerican ruins themselves; *Petrocoatl* is a brilliant continuation of and modern-day takeoff on such images, at the same time warning us of the danger un-

10. This and the following quotes are all from the lecture, either from Tejada himself or from the artists.

checked industry poses to the sites of ancient cultures and humanity's survival.

Another of the artists whose work Roberto shows us and who moves me deeply is Adriana Corral. She takes as her point of departure the Universal Declaration of Human Rights, a document adopted in 1948 by the United Nations General Assembly that affirms the inherent dignity owed all members of the human family. Copies of the document are available free online, and Corral incinerated one and incorporated the burnt paper ashes into art composed of what she describes as "resilient matter" and "movement through breath, movement through pain, movement through uncertainty." Her art honors the great number of women who have been raped, tortured, and murdered in Ciudad Juárez recorded just since 1993.

There was so much in Tejada's lecture for me to take in that I played the video several times and then asked him to send me his written script, which he was kind enough to do. All the artists were revelations, their art brilliantly contesting the brutal systems of oppression that plague all people of color and other marginalized groups. These are survivors, not victims, whose art is their resistance and who choose to express their creative power and response through their creativity.

There are also a couple of artists whose work affects me in ways that make me extremely uncomfortable and lead me to question whether I consider it art. I don't think of art as something passive, agreeable, easy to look at. I am willing to be challenged, even rudely so, by work that reflects unjust or grotesque situations. But I guess I am enough of a traditionalist that I think of art as something to which I love coming back, appreciate seeing again and again. Angel Lartigue's work, in dealing with horrific deaths along the south Texas border, triggers memories in me which I find very difficult to deal with. Over the past twenty-two years, more than

3,253 people have lost their lives attempting to enter the United States across this border. Lartigue researched the material process of decomposing bodies in Brooks County, where the number of recorded migrant deaths exceeds that of any other Texas county over the last three decades. In her work, she uses material from several of those bodies. Was it that material that so unnerved me?

When I arrived in Nicaragua shortly after the Sandinista victory of 1979, one of the collective tasks in which I took part was the removal of the corpses of young soldiers who had been shot down by the side of country roads and hurriedly buried in shallow makeshift graves. We were charged with moving those bodies to more permanent resting places in cemeteries. I will never forget the stench of decomposing human flesh; it is like no other odor and lingers in cellular memory. Viewing Lartigue's work evokes vivid memories. I could smell those bodies of young Nicaraguan soldiers again, although the experience is several decades old.

This challenged my idea of what art is. I couldn't imagine visiting Lartigue's work in a gallery or museum, let alone having it in my home. I expressed my feelings to Tejada and asked how he defines art. He wrote back that he finds use in "art writer Molly Nesbit's understanding of art as 'an open site' and 'a way of working.' In this sense artworks intersect with philosophy and other forms of human activity that seek 'to grasp the torrent of incongruity, the injustices, the torn hopes, the achievements....'" And he went on to say: "because art can prompt degrees of pleasure or unease, art philosopher Peter Osborne views art as a set of historical practices that name a problem expressing that 'crisis in form' as expressions that can please or disturb, but at any rate, yes, with qualities that cannot simply be reduced to a claim or message."

Tejada's lecture didn't only provoke these notes. I realized my definition of what art is continues to fluctuate, that no matter what position I take I feel like a devil's advocate even to myself. So, I shared the lecture with my friend, US American painter Greg Smith, hoping we might explore the issue together. Greg and I often discuss art, politics, and life in general. The following is a partial transcript of the emails we exchanged about the lecture:

> Margaret: The anti-colonialist non-binary and queer Latinx art that Roberto shares ... left me pondering what art is. While I found all his examples, and the performances, extraordinarily powerful, I couldn't imagine having some of them in my home, looking at them daily.... Perhaps I am too accustomed to thinking of art as something that can shock and/or shake us up but that nevertheless we can enjoy seeing in museums, public places, and in our own homes. I can appreciate the messages—visual as well as implied—that all the artists transmitted. And I was left with the same astonishment/gratitude you have. But I couldn't imagine revisiting some of it on a regular basis. It's interesting that you mention the work that takes The Universal Declaration of Human Rights as its point of departure. That was one of the examples I was most able to relate to without the barrier I've just described.
>
> Greg: I share your feelings about being powerfully moved by the work Roberto highlighted in his talk, but I do not feel it is art. I feel it is a very high level of activist performance—necessary, educational, and moving to varying degrees. As you know, my views on art—fine art—are strict and "classical" for lack of a more appropriate term that really does not adhere to a term—other than art is separate from everything else, primarily separate from the utility of life. Fine art is radical precisely because it is useless. It is the

one thing we do that has nothing to do with anything other than the silent, still object itself. And I do mean object. Fine art is a physical thing—actual thing—that humans make. Performance, music, and film are forms of art. But they are not high art. They depend upon a prescribed narrative or audience and, as such, are tied to a certain utility of entertainment. While we live in a very pluralistic time—when everything is mistakenly termed art—when everyone is considered an artist—nothing could be further from the truth of art. Art is never an entertainment or pastime for boredom. It redeems us by existing solely beyond the banal. We see art. We cannot say it.

Margaret: I understand, and to a certain extent agree with, what you say. Your phrase "We see art. We cannot say it" resonates especially. I have never liked the term "high art," though. And I continue to wonder about creative manifestations that are political in nature but have that magical quality art possesses. In terms of visual art, I am thinking about Goya's war sketches, Picasso's *Guernica*, Leandro Katz's *Catherwood Project*, the construction about the two trees by Sabra Moore that we have hanging on our living room wall, or Barbara's roller prints made on pages of the Bible, among many others. Then there are Bach's music, Frank Lloyd Wright's architecture, Luis Buñuel's or Sergei Eisenstein's films. In my opinion all these go way beyond entertainment. None of them are separate from the utility of life. They are not useless. Precisely the opposite. They manage to speak to issues and/or emotions that deeply affect us, while retaining that almost indefinable something that—to me—makes them art.

To further explore the question of what art is, and because Greg's rejection of art as anything but the object itself is seductive to me, I turned to a fascinating source, Rika Burnham.[11] A theorist, curator, and practitioner of art museum education, she writes: "In the decades I tried to understand the practice and theory of dialogical engagement in the art museum, I had two great realizations. The first was the idea that questions, any questions, no matter how 'open,' are impositions, and the second was ... to leave the discussion open at the end rather than closing it with a grand finale." Perhaps the idea that we can answer the question "what is art?" is itself another way of trying to close the discussion with a grand finale.

As we've seen, a great many thinkers throughout history have expressed themselves on the nature and/or meaning of art, each influenced by their culture and time. Still, we cannot always be sure that a manifestation we see as art was intended as such. For example, we refer to the images chiseled and painted on cave walls throughout the world as "rock art" but have no way of knowing what they were to those who made them. The written concept of art is itself relatively new, only a few thousand years old out of the many millennia of humanity's history. What we see as ancient art may in fact have been maps, messaging, memory, storytelling, or something else.

This is an issue I'm still pondering. In time, I may feel differently about specific works. I've been able to open myself to ideas that were once unimaginable to me, such as the internet, GPS, space travel, gender transition for those born into the wrong bodies, and changes in the use of personal pronouns to accommodate such identities. Art

11. Burnham is quoted as interviewed by Pablo Helguera in "Renaissance Riddles" on his Substack, *Beautiful Eccentrics*, February 22, 2024.

reflects life and the ideas and experiences it gives us, and I would like to think I am also open to a changing perception of what art is.

Perhaps the best way of exploring what art is, is always to continue the conversation rather than expressing some immutable truth.

Integrity and Art

"How does meaning get into the image?
Where does it end? And if it ends,
what is there beyond?"

—Roland Barthes

INTEGRITY OR ITS LACK can separate what endures from what doesn't. I believe this is as true about art as it is about other areas of endeavor. Artistic expression transmits our most meaningful maps, courageous imaginations, and deepest values. It is often argued that it is what separates us from other animals, thus defining our humanity. I am not at all sure that other animals don't make art, but I agree that what we humans make represents our most profound intellectual and emotional expression. Still, describing integrity in art can be complicated. The Roland Barthes quote I use as an epigraph to this text may be applied to literature as well as to visual art. Meaning and creativity can seem mysteriously separate or brilliantly of a piece.

I don't mean that a text necessarily lacks integrity if it's created by a racist, sexist, or fascist, or that we can't admire a painting or sculpture by someone with whose values we disagree. That we should refuse to view Woody Allen's films because he is accused of sexually abusing his stepdaughter, or dismiss Picasso's art because of his flagrant misogyny. Work created by imperfect artists or writers may still be beautiful or meaningful or push us to entertain ideas that expand our consciousness. There is always something that sparks our imagination.

I *do* mean that an unencumbered passion for justice imbues art with an element that adds to its overall value and impact. It can launch us into an orbit of noble ideals, even encourage us to act in ways that embody those ideals. It may be argued that objects of literature and art exist as unique entities in and of themselves, that they are situated beyond the philosophical or political stance of those who create them. While I accept this at the most elemental level, I sense another energy, an almost immaterial materiality that is present.

It can sometimes be difficult to separate a poem or piece of art from the consciousness and conduct of the poet or visual artist who created it. This is equally true for musicians, actors, photographers, dancers, architects, and others. We've all known of painters who early in their careers hit on a mode of expression that gained them broad appeal. Rather than continue to explore, the artists in question spend the rest of their lives repeating the gesture that brought them fame and fortune. An example is the Mexican José Luis Cuevas, who had initial success drawing a certain style of monstrous figure and kept on repeating it throughout his career. The more authentic painters—or practitioners of any of the other art forms—will continue to explore new forms, dismantle boundaries, experiment with other possibilities. Leonardo da Vinci and William Shakespeare come to mind.

Conversely, other artists and writers may continue with a gesture that has evaded commercial success but is true to their vision, need, and desire. An innate integrity may lead them to make the same statement again and again, despite its failure to bring recognition. Barbara Rose, who edited the painter Ad Reinhardt's writings, asked him why he kept publishing the same text over and over in different magazines. He said, "Because they haven't understood it yet." This may be true of many artists or writers who repeat themselves not because they've hit on something that has brought them acclaim or money but for the opposite reason.

Reinhardt is an extraordinary example of this. He was one of the Abstract Expressionists who gained acclaim mid-twentieth century, but unlike Jackson Pollock, Franz Kline, and Willem de Kooning, whose powerful gestures with paint came to be known as Action Painting, his mature work was quiet: large black canvases in which layers of blue-black, brown-black, and other blacks produced an inner light from a surface many might have described as uniform. Reinhardt is remembered as a man of integrity in his life as well as in his art. He was a Communist and marched for justice alongside much younger artists. He joined Betty Parsons' gallery in 1946 and was still there when he died, in contrast with many other well-known artists she represented who eventually left because she wasn't getting them the sales they wanted. "Ad would complain she wasn't selling his work, but he knew perfectly well she showed art for love not money and ... he liked that."[1]

Rose asks: "Suppose Ad had not died when he was only 54 but had lived as long as de Kooning. Do you think he

1. This quote and the following observations about Reinhardt (1913–1967) are from a conversation titled "Ping/Pong: Lucy Lippard and Barbara Rose Talk About Reinhardt." The conversation took place years ago but was published by The Brooklyn Rail in 2023.

would have continued to paint only black paintings? What do you think?" Lucy Lippard responds: "Such an interesting question. He had in a sense backed himself into a corner, a corner where he was relatively content and making amazing art." No one can know, of course, but Lippard and Rose (and, I would argue, anyone who loves Ad Reinhardt's work) agree about the man's integrity—in his art and in his life.

Authenticity should not be confused with integrity. One can be authentic to oneself even when one may be devious, lazy, self-centered, elitist, racist, misogynist, narrow-minded, mean-spirited, overly competitive and ambitious, bitter, divisive, or in possession of any number of other negative traits. Integrity is something else. It means being true to oneself *and* to ideals of respect for the earth and its inhabitants.

And then there is impartiality, a faux attitude that has been vastly overrated in the United States. Impartiality posits that it is important to represent an issue from all angles. But all angles aren't equal. The point of view of a fascist is diametrically opposed to that of someone who believes in equality. One who hunts animals as trophies holds beliefs that are different from those held by people who love and respect them. Those who make a living from war and those who struggle for peace are at opposite ends of the moral spectrum.

Impartiality can go a long way toward watering down integrity, moving us away from a principled stance in the name of what passes for fairness. Commercial media makes a claim to impartiality, even when the subject being examined clearly demands taking a position. And our culture has found ingenious ways of twisting language so that a given discourse may pretend to represent something very different from what is said. An impartial stance generally means that cowardice situates the work conveniently in the mainstream, hopes to impress the broadest number of people, or simply seeks to avoid conflict. Artists always have a point of view, even when they claim not to.

We might add rigidity to the list. Although I believe integrity to be one of our highest values, it's important not to become entrenched in positions we believe are right. Listening to those with whom we disagree and being willing to entertain ideas different from our own can be enlightening. If we hide behind a particular position, we deny ourselves access to other experiences and ideas.

So, there is authenticity, impartiality, rigidity, and integrity: each representing a different but interrelated character trait. They may intersect, but integrity is foremost on my mind, especially now when what US Americans once considered our core values seem so prone to erosion.

If an artist can have integrity or not, this is also true of those who write about art. Honest criticism is lacking in our culture; its practitioners give us rare gifts. Reviews are too often published to make or destroy a reputation rather than to probe the cultural history that produced a work or explore the ideas and feelings it may evoke and examine the methods employed. Ordinary viewers and readers may be equally reticent to express their honest opinions. Reluctant to say what we think, "it's interesting" has become a response of choice: bland and meaningless. This nod to conformity and good manners also makes it easier to stray from a position of integrity.

At a poetry reading not long ago, I was disappointed to hear the poet say that on a recent tour of our state's small towns she had been careful not to reveal her political position. Clearly, she was suggesting that she didn't believe her audiences sophisticated enough to receive her ideas. Her condescending attitude was disappointing and spoke to me of a lack of integrity. I found this particularly troubling because we are living in such a dangerous time; throughout the world we are dealing with life-and-death issues that need to be addressed fearlessly. I was reminded of Fidel Castro's comment in the early years of the Cuban revolution, when he warned against speaking down to the masses and said that instead the cultural level of those masses had to be raised so that they would be able to receive, engage with, and contribute to the most advanced ideas and cultural innovation.

Integrity can also manifest itself outside the work itself, in a person's conduct: the size of their ego, how they treat others, what they are willing to do to get ahead, where they draw a line they aren't willing to cross. There is a delicate balance between putting oneself out there, hoping to communicate through one's talent, and promoting oneself in ways that lack integrity. And while we have sadly come to expect this lack of integrity in our dealings with the corporate world, it is jarring to confront it in venues we somehow assume should lead by example—such as government, religious institutions, the academy, and our many overlapping art scenes.

In our work, artists and writers reflect life around us or offer an alternative vision. Integrity is important in terms of the reality we project and the values it embodies.

For authors, integrity may be at stake when someone asks us to write an introduction to a book, a review, or even just a back-cover blurb. What do we really think? Can we in all honesty recommend the work? We may be tempted to comply because the author is a friend and, although we don't like what we read, cannot bring ourselves to say no. We may agree in the hope that the person asking will return the favor. Art reflects life just as life reflects art. My friend, the Canadian writer and social commentator Stan Persky, wrote that "life's only twin is art." I think this is true in more ways than we imagine.

I began taking myself seriously as a poet in my early twenties. In my struggle to acquire the necessary skills, I was immensely appreciative of several generous mentors. Their patience and teachings are still with me. These people and others modeled making art as something legitimate, worthy of full attention and lifetime effort. They were the very embodiment of integrity. Looking back, I often find myself wondering what these and other accomplished thinkers and artists saw in me. Clearly a potential I didn't yet see in myself.

My first poems were embarrassing. As I struggled to develop my voice, I came upon younger writers beginning their journeys. When I saw promise, I always tried to open doors and share opportunities. I rejected occasional urges to save some useful piece of information for myself, perhaps naively believing that talent and experience would win out, but certainly understanding that selfishness negates integrity. Today I devote a great deal of energy to encouraging younger writers, translating their work, putting them in touch with publishing outlets, writing letters of recommendation for scholarships or grants, and occasionally even aiding in editing a manuscript. This is how I pay forward the help I received when I was starting out.

For visual artists, museums and galleries are frequently the venues in which their work makes its way in the world. My wife Barbara has steadfastly resisted that system. Instead, she shows her work in alternative spaces and to folks who come to the house and ask to see it. She creates one-of-a-kind calling cards and distributes them freely. And when we make our annual visit to Naropa University's Summer Writing Program, she brings dozens of small drawings or prints which she affixes to the walls and tells people to take them if they wish. Barbara says that making art is her way of contributing to putting the world back together; she does it because she must.

Sadly, our country doesn't support the artist or writer to the degree that many others do. Most creative people must work at something else to sustain themselves. In many ways, then, being able to operate according to one's own values is a luxury. It is still, however, a choice.

For a poet or writer, the public sphere includes readings (these days often held on Zoom), publication in magazines, contests with entry fees, and, eventually, finding a publisher. Consultants and agents of different sorts are frequently part of the mix. I specifically mention Zoom events because, since the Covid pandemic, they have become increasingly popular and can bring an audience from across the globe. On Zoom, my poetry has reached people in India, Ireland, Italy, Australia, Finland, and South Africa, throughout Latin America, and across the US and Canada: a deeply satisfying experience.

Writers still trying to get a foot in the publishing door submit their work only to face one rejection after another. In desperation, they may finally decide to self-publish. The corporate world always has as its primary goal that of making a profit from such writers. It almost always disappoints in that it charges a lot and promotes very little. In recent years, of course, the internet has changed this landscape. Today some writers choose to put their work online because they want it to be freely accessible. There is a vast network of writers and publishers who believe in free access to culture and information. Through several open-access platforms, they are taking a principled stand against mega corporations such as Amazon and Google that exploit their workers as well as creators of content.

I self-published my first two slim poetry books. All the rest—and there have been more than two hundred to date—have been produced by publishing houses where I didn't have to pay for the privilege: from the occasional commercial house to university presses, leftist and feminist projects, and independents that commit themselves to making available texts they consider important beyond fad or profitability.

I've been immensely fortunate that half a dozen brilliant editors and book designers have taken me on and made beautiful homes for my work. And when another poet or writer whose work I find exciting asks me to suggest a press, I am always willing to connect them to one, often writing letters of introduction and urging my editors to read their manuscripts.

I used to try for some of the big writing grants, believing I might have a chance to do nothing but my own work for a year or two. I never won any and eventually gave up. Although I came up in a misogynist society—or maybe because I did—I also believed I could "have it all," and as a result I raised four children, worked full time to support us, and threw myself into the struggle for social change, all while developing myself as a writer. It's only been since formal retirement, in my so-called "old age," that I've had the luxury of writing full time. I'm keenly aware of how much my work has improved as a result. Creating is so much more than simply producing a text. It requires the proverbial room of one's own, research, study, and the absence of other overwhelming distractions and responsibilities. It takes time and a certain freedom of mind to nurture imagination and then get out of the way and allow the work to show up.

My writing often goes against current trends or resists a popular point of view. I insist that the personal is political and that the political must take the personal into account. I was among the first in the United States to publish a collection of poetry and prose that was explicitly about a childhood experience of incest.[2] I believe that secrets harm us, but mystery and imagination are necessary. And I am drawn to uncomfortable subjects such as religion, politics, money, anger, human tics, lying, the perils of memory and danger of its erasure, obesity, rebellion, and the exceptions to

2. *This Is About Incest.* Firebrand Books, 1987.

any contrived norm. I ask unpopular questions and propose unpopular answers. While I vehemently support #MeToo and other movements for justice, I also look at instances in which those movements have gone too far, hurting people who don't deserve to be written off. My poems are "too political" for some, "too personal" for others, two labels I reject. They refuse to echo any of the many trends that have been popular throughout my writing life.

My generation in the United States was deeply affected by the chill of McCarthyism. The anti-Communist witch hunt destroyed friends and colleagues, deprived us of unknown numbers of works of art, and created a timidity among anyone who held progressive beliefs. Its residual aura made many writers I knew fearful of expressing ideas that might be considered contrary to the established order.

Fortunately, I moved to Latin America in my mid-twenties and remained there (in Mexico, Cuba, and Nicaragua) for almost a quarter century. This was good for my creative life because it not only opened me to rich millennial cultures and their peoples, but also put me in touch with writers and artists who believe one can write—or paint or make music or work in whatever genre—about anything and everything. I was able to escape the subtle and not-so-subtle coercion that burdened many of my US contemporaries in the wake of the McCarthy witch hunt. A deeply embedded resistance to censorship and self-censorship took root in me early on.

In Mexico, where I lived from 1961 to 1969, Sergio Mondragón and I met at a writing salon made up of poets from various latitudes.[3] Reading our work to one another,

3. In the early 1960s, Surrealist poet Philip Lamantia and his wife Lucille hosted a nightly salon in Mexico City's Colonia Cuauhtémoc. Nicaraguan Ernesto Cardenal, Mexicans Juan Bañuelos and Homero Aridijis, Chilean Raquel Jodorowsky, and Sergio and I were among

we quickly realized the need for good translation. We embarked on what in retrospect seems like an almost impossible adventure: founding, editing, distributing, and raising the money for *El Corno Emplumado / The Plumed Horn. El Corno*, as its readers still call it, was an entirely independent book-sized quarterly journal that ran for eight years and published work in Spanish and English, eventually showcasing more than seven hundred writers and artists from thirty-five countries. Their vast differences in terms of culture, style, political persuasion, and individual voice opened me to worlds I might not have accessed had I remained in the US.

The magazine prided itself on not publishing work by people simply because they were our friends or well-known. Neither did we limit ourselves to a particular trend or style. Our integrity resided in accepting work of excellent quality and rejecting what wasn't, or what espoused authoritarian, classist, racist, or sexist views. We honored experimentation. And we designed our format with the work in mind, choosing vertical or horizontal placement to show it off to its best advantage.

Many years later, during the first court trial of my immigration case,[4] the government lawyer asked pointedly: "Is it true, Ms. Randall, that you edited a magazine in the

those who attended.

4. In 1967, married to Mondragón and with two more children, I acquired Mexican citizenship to better help support my growing family. When I returned to the US in 1984 and applied for residency, I was ordered deported based on opinions expressed in seven of my books. I was charged under the ideological exclusion clause of the 1952 McCarran-Walter Immigration and Nationality Act. With the help of excellent lawyers and a great deal of public support, I won my case in 1989 and was granted not only residency but reinstatement of citizenship. For a detailed discussion of the case, see *Coming Home: Peace Without Complacency*, West End Press, 1990.

1960s that published Communists?" She failed to mention that *El Corno* had also published work by religious mystics, surrealists, guerrilla poets, students, indigenous writers, carpenters, sailors, academics, well-known authors, and incipient voices. Living in different countries among different peoples is always enormously enriching. For an artist it is particularly so.

Perhaps it is having known so many different sorts of artists from so many different histories and cultures, and having participated in several movements for social change myself, that has enabled me to spot the poseur and introduced me to an integrity and authenticity contrary to the elitist, apolitical, self-involved, often male-dominated norms that exist in this country's MFA programs, particularly in the 1970s and '80s but sadly continuing to this day. I believe my discovery of feminism was also key. It taught me about power as a political category and opened me to many exceptional women poets (and visual artists, painters, sculptors, dancers, actors, photographers, architects, composers, etc.) who were beginning to demolish the gendered barriers to publishing and exhibiting that have yet to completely disappear.

Art is also memory, sometimes the only memory left in societies that intentionally write a history that distorts their legacy and struggles. Censoring art erases memory. Integrity is sometimes the only thing that preserves the memory that tells us who we were, are, and can be.

Writing this in my late eighties, I've naturally thought about what will happen to my work when I'm gone. My participation in several important sociocultural moments, my friendships with other writers and artists of my time, and my own work lend my archive historical interest. My manuscripts, photographic negatives and prints, correspondence, and ephemera have been useful to scholars in several research areas. My papers reside at the Center for Southwest Research at my hometown University of New Mexico.

I trust its curators to make it available according to my wishes.[5]

But what about posthumous publication? Not wanting to burden my wife or children with those decisions, I needed a literary executor. I am immensely fortunate to be able to count on my good friend Katherine M. Hedeen, who is fluent in English and Spanish, knowledgeable about the Latin American and US poetry scenes, and, perhaps equally important, young enough that she is likely to outlive me by many years. I'm not worried about the income my work may generate after my death; it hasn't brought me much up to now. What concerns me is where it might be published and to what ends. I want to think it will continue to be used in line with my beliefs and in support of positions important to me.

From the time he was a child, one of my grandsons demonstrated a degree of integrity that surprised his elders. Not surprisingly, he is one of the artists in our family. His integrity seemed exaggerated at times, and had he not been such a well-liked and friendly young boy he might have been isolated by his peers. He was always sensitive to poverty and hardship, became a vegetarian for moral reasons, befriended and aided kids from difficult backgrounds, and routinely refused privileges not available to everyone. For many of his formative years he wouldn't even ride in a car when others were limited to using public transportation, admonished his parents for having a summer place as well as their city apartment, and preferred staying home to accompanying his family on trips. (He knew these were privileges not everyone can have.) As a teenager, he participated in a successful movement to shut down his city's zoo on the grounds that

5. I have directed that my texts and images be freely accessible except for seven decades of personal journals, which will be closed to the public until thirty years after my death.

its small cages were cruel to the animals. Eventually, life tempered some of these positions. But, now in his thirties and a father himself, he continues to have enormous integrity.

Perhaps art's more abstract nature makes associating it with issues of integrity more difficult, but I think there is evidence to the contrary.

T. S. Eliot was a traditionalist, Ezra Pound had fascist leanings, José Luis Borges was doggedly right-wing, yet these writers moved beyond reactionary ideologies to create works of value. Their political views are contrary to mine, but their writing is exquisite, sometimes magical. It is part of a canon I respect. The Peruvian Mario Vargas Llosa espouses right-wing political ideas but, interestingly, his novels embody values and a sensibility with which those of us on the left identify. The contradiction between the author's political positions and his writing is hard to categorize. Should we assume that his true passion is in his work, his political maneuvering an opportunistic tic? Difficult to say. And then there is Pablo Neruda, a Chilean Communist whose poetry soars but whose autobiography shows him to have been an unrepentant misogynist. The relationship between artists and their work is often complex.

But then I think about César Vallejo, Nazim Hikmet, Walter Benjamin, Mario Benedetti, Mark Behr, Barbara Kingsolver, Antón Arrufat, Raul Zurita, Audre Lorde, Adrienne Rich, Juan Gelman, Paul Monette, Susan Sherman, Anne Waldman, V. B. Price, and countless others, whose integrity and ability to cross proscribed boundaries allowed them to produce work that says more and says it better. I would argue that these latter writers will be remembered for as long as literature has readers. More importantly, I believe that their work changes values. What they have written not only moves us deeply; it plants seeds that help us see the world and ourselves in new ways.

This text is meant as an invitation to conversation, food for thought and discussion, rather than as a list of absolutes. I'll close by reiterating a few of my personal convictions. Integrity in art embodies values that should be transparent, an innate understanding of right and wrong not based on imposed dictates such as religious or political dogma. It embraces a profound honesty, genuine love of life, and a belief in equality and justice for all peoples. It demonstrates a passion to live one's values, for curiosity, fair-mindedness, and generosity of spirit. Perhaps most importantly, it is a willingness to follow one's beliefs to their ultimate consequences. Despite all explanations, excuses, justifications or lies, these values are self-evident. It doesn't take an educated mind to spot them. How we discern them may be difficult to explain, but we can learn to trust our instincts.

Imagination Looks in the Mirror

BETWEEN THE AGES OF AROUND SIX AND TEN, I had four imaginary friends. They lived in a closet-like space beneath the stairs of my childhood home, a place I often retreated to as a refuge from the uncertainties of life with adults. My imaginary friends were a man named Mr. Beeuf who worked in a factory and left the house each morning with a domed black lunch box like the one my father took with him to work, Miss Level who was a nurse, a young man named Camp who rode a motorcycle, and a young woman named Girlie. Recently I learned that my oldest grandchild, Lía, also had four imaginary friends as a child. I wondered about the number four, and also if her children have such invented characters in their lives. Imagining and inventing the sorts of companions they need is a privilege of youth.

In our societies, to carry into adulthood the sort of imagination that invents friends would be considered mental illness—except in the case of poets, who demand and receive all manner of dispensation. It's not infrequent that poets create alternate personae, poets as well, who have different concerns and write in different styles. The Portuguese poet Fernando Pessoa (1888–1935) was known for this; he gave voice to seventy alternate poetic personalities, some of them women. Toward the end of his life, the Salvadoran Roque Dalton invented five imaginary poets, one of whom was female. One was a young seminary student, another a laborer. Each wrote from his or her unique background and perspective.

Imagination is nurtured through experience. Children who grow up in families where they are exposed to art, music, literature, theater, and other creative manifestations—especially when these come from other cultures as well as their own—are more likely to develop imagination than those who are constrained by the routine and prosaic. I would say that imagination is the capacity to think beyond the confines of lived experience, envisioning that experience extending itself outward in unlimited, unexpected, and magical ways. It is the passion to insist on a vision even when it defies common understanding or socially acceptable behavior. The impossible becomes possible.

We may take a thought and run with it, even when we are unsure of where it will take us. We may gaze on a landscape and imagine it altered in color, perspective, motion, time, space. We may see it open, move, brighten, transform, fade. We may embroider an event to become something else entirely or imbue it with qualities others don't perceive. We may be driven to create what others cannot visualize. There is risk and possibility. Vincent van Gogh's genius lay precisely in his ability to paint the world as he saw it rather than how others did. Amadeus Mozart, even as a child, heard musical notes in ways others did not. Great architects base their work on conceptions they alone envision. Great chefs imagine flavor combinations that wouldn't occur to more mundane palates. Great writers invent whole new ways of using language.

This is how vision emerges from the psyche and becomes creativity, invention, important scientific discovery, an artistic masterpiece, or mind-altering text. Memory is central here, because imagination tends to be layered: a twist of the mind with the proclivity to go where few venture, engendered by an experience that for most people would be unthinkable. By the same token, there is a tragic link between the ways in which society systematically erases memory and the stifling of the sort of imagination that can lead to a practice that prioritizes creativity.

When imagination is accompanied by discipline and persistence, the outcome is more powerful. If people with highly developed imaginations conceive of an idea and then stay with it as it evolves in whatever way it will, their efforts can leave an indelible mark. They may have a preconceived notion of where it will lead them, but not always. They aren't cowed or deterred by suggestions that they conform to society's idea of how they should act or what they are free to create.

Imagination comes in many sizes and shapes. It may be the intimate product of a minimalist artist whose paintings or constructions become environments and whose practice is one with the work. It may reside in certain types of land art in which the artist alters the terrain so it may speak in a different register—most often ephemerally. It may be as vast as Raven Chacon's "Voiceless Mass" or Jon Batiste's "American Symphony," musical scores that are as inclusive as they are monumental. It may be the gesture of the unidentified man who stood alone, with a single flower in his hand, before fifty-nine tanks in Beijing's Tiananmen Square on June 5, 1989, the day after China's massacre of hundreds of protesters. It may be the creations of a poet who writes alone her entire life, oblivious to fame or even to whether anyone will ever hear her voice. A scientist might dream of making the discovery that will eradicate a terrible illness or be content with deciphering a small piece of a much larger puzzle. It's all imagination and it's all important to moving humanity forward. It isn't about how loud or soft, insistent, or subtle it may be.

If Hypatia of Alexandria hadn't imagined she had every right to possess knowledge and to teach... If Galileo, despite ominous threat, hadn't kept looking in his telescope... If Michelangelo hadn't been able to envision the ceiling of the Sistine Chapel alive with his painting or the Mexican muralists understood they needed whole walls for the stories they had to tell... If Leonardo hadn't given full expression to a mind that soared in invention as well as art, describing that expression in mirror as well as straightforward imagery... If Benjamin Franklin hadn't envisioned the leap from lightning to electricity... If Salk hadn't imagined the vaccine that would leave polio sputtering... If Dante... If Shakespeare... If Bach... If Thelonious... If Raven Chacón... If Ai Wei Wei... If Jon Batiste... If Rigoberta Menchú... If Judd... If Haring... If Basquiat... If J. K. Rowling... If Julie Taymor... If Malala Yousafzai... If Greta Thunberg...

If these possessors of great imagination, and so many others like them, had lacked the courage to follow their dreams, the world would be a very different place. Think of Britain's role in the Second World War without the brilliance and unfailing persistence of Alan Turing; the genius decoder Enigma would not have existed to help defeat the Nazis. Imagine all the women during that same war who used their privileged mathematical minds as human calculators to track weapon trajectories.

Imagination can also lead in unexpected directions.

The 2023 film *Oppenheimer* resituates us in one of recent history's most dramatic events. The Manhattan Project, a secret working group of physicists headed by Robert

Oppenheimer and located in northern New Mexico, developed nuclear fission at the request of the US government. They aimed their imaginations at a goal that risked setting on fire nothing less than our atmosphere and destroying life on earth.[1] Joseph Rotblat started out at the Project but left on grounds of conscience in late 1944 when it became clear Germany was not close to developing its own nuclear bomb—the only scientist to leave the project for moral reasons. But there was another physicist who refused to take part from the beginning. She was Lise Meitner, who, in fact, co-discovered nuclear fission along with Oppenheimer. When asked to join the team, she refused. Hers was a powerful imagination that included a healthy quota of political responsibility; she knew weaponization would have to be the end result of the work at Los Alamos. Historians have largely written her out of the story. She is not even mentioned in the film. This is undoubtedly due in part to the gender discrimination that is still so prevalent in the arts as well as in society generally. But I can't help thinking that omitting her was also due to a lack of imagination, and that to have included her would have shown the moral courage imagination so often brings.

1. *Oppenheimer* is based on the 2005 biography *American Prometheus* by Kal Bird and Martin J. Sherwin. The film was written and directed by Christopher Nolan. It stars Cillian Murphy as J. Robert Oppenheimer, the American theoretical physicist credited with being the "father of the atomic bomb" for his role in the Manhattan Project, the World War II effort that developed the first nuclear weapons. The film contextualizes the story within the McCarthy period and climaxes in a series of hearings at which revocation of Oppenheimer's Q clearance is considered in light of his previous Communist ties. Throughout the film, opinions about the moral implications of developing the bomb are weighed, with a particularly intriguing conversation between Oppenheimer and Einstein in which the latter firmly declares his opposition. Comprehensive as the film is, however, it leaves out much key material.

We tend to think of those who possess great imagination as unique human beings, innately different from the rest of us. But everything points to the fact that most of us are born with endless curiosity and wonder. Children throughout the world show an astonishing ability to think creatively and even at very young ages to ask questions or make drawings that astonish. When their minds are allowed to flourish, their imaginations know no bounds and they travel to extraordinary places. It is society itself that kills this instinct, insisting on controlling us by trying to get us to conform and confine ourselves within prescribed limits that dull our edges and destroy our visions. As children we are coerced into filling pre-outlined coloring books, painting according to the numbers. When we are older, we are asked to answer multiple-choice questions rather than develop our own ability to think critically.

Some cultures do encourage imagination from an early age. The Latin American countries in which I've lived place a higher value on it than we do here in the United States; many Asian and African cultures do as well. Bali is a nation where imagination flourishes; it is closely linked to the dominant religion. Still, in most places when children display a real disposition for the arts or pass their time thinking up far-fetched inventions, their parents tend to be amused or even proud of their ingenuity when they are young but are likely to discourage them as they get older. They tell them to study something that will help them get ahead or advise them to "get a real job" because imagination is linked to daydreaming and creativity isn't considered a legitimate pursuit. Many would-be artists swallow their instincts when faced with social pressures to conform.

Despite all the progress toward equality we have made in recent years, we still live in a highly gendered society. The patriarchy has very different expectations of men and women and affords each vastly different opportunities.

Important stereotypes persist. Men are assumed to operate from a position of logic and reason; women are thought to possess more intuition and imagination—but these supposedly female qualities lack social value. Because it is assumed they will find a man to support them and the children they may have, women early on may be allowed to explore their creativity more freely than men. Ironically, later those same women tend to sideline or give up their creative endeavors precisely because they are expected to serve their husbands and children.

Those who manage to escape society's assumptions about how much they should be allowed to let their imaginations run free frequently do so at great personal risk. They may not be able to conform, are driven to pursue their passion but don't deal well with other areas of life, and as a result are often dubbed *mentally ill* or *impossibly radical* because they insist on expressing qualities the majority has lost.

I have known several such people. I remember an artist named Carlos Coffeen Serpas,[2] whose marvelous drawings we published in *El Corno Emplumado*. Tormented, he lived with his mother in a single room in the slums of Mexico City. He could barely respond when spoken to, but his genius shone in his art. Who knows how he might have flourished had society provided a safety net for people like himself. Around the same time, I met Beltrán Morales, a young Nicaraguan poet who was bipolar and subject to frightening episodes of manic depression during which it was impossible for him to hold a job or function socially. Much later, when I reconnected with him in Nicaragua during the initial years of the Sandinista revolution, he was married, able to give his imagination free rein, and was working on an endless manuscript. The revolutionary

2. Serpas (1932–1988) was a little-known Mexican surrealist artist. His mother, the Salvadoran poet Liliana Serpas, was much better known.

government provided a living stipend for artists and writers like him who were burdened with conditions that made normal life difficult. All Beltrán needed to excel was that help. It made all the difference.[3]

There is such tension between full-throated imagination and our social constraints that people often struggle to function within their imagined paradigms. On the one hand, they are constantly moved to stretch themselves to the extent of their impulses, or beyond. On the other, they are just as constantly being pulled back to the safety of "normal" behavior. For the imaginatively driven, life is not about survival but about exploring every possibility, taking every idea as far as they are able.

Writers of science fiction use their imaginations to create worlds of the future, often post-apocalyptic or technologically advanced, with such elements as cyber-humans, gender bending, voiceless communication, interplanetary travel, or dystopian landscapes left barren by war or climate devastation. Some, like *Star Trek*, imagine universes with hybrid civilizations. Their inhabitants may possess superpowers. Others, like *The Hunger Games*,[4] warn us that if we continue as we are, we are headed for a dangerous self-defeating world. This is a genre that ranges from the cliched to the extraordinarily complex. It may parody current values or foretell situations destined to become reality.

3. Morales (1945–1986) died of problems linked to the medications he took. In his brief life, he published several volumes of poetry, essays, and literary criticism. After his death, his *Complete Poems* was released.

4. *The Hunger Games*, first a trilogy by Suzanne Collins, then films featuring Jennifer Lawrence in the starring role of Katniss Everdeen, address a world gone mad in the logical extension of today's sociopolitical madness. Katniss is a brilliant role model for young women combatting the ugliest greed and criminality with courage and morality.

During the Covid pandemic, in 2022, I suddenly found myself exploring a genre that wasn't typical for me. I had always written poetry, essay, and oral history. I began writing short stories and soon had a collection of twenty-three.[5] Although some have classified them as science fiction, my stories don't involve futurist worlds or supernatural powers. Rather, they are situated in the present or near-present when, nevertheless, strange things begin to happen. Action may shift subtly. Time may go backwards. Places lose certain features or disappear completely. Characters display hidden abilities. My imagination is interested in a world that is familiar until something changes, and that change presents us with unexpected options—much like the world we currently inhabit.

Science fiction often presents us with situations and characters that project our greatest dilemmas by transporting us to a futuristic realm in which superpowers enable us to imagine solutions impossible today. But we also suffer situations possible to address in the present if we are willing to imagine change. Sometimes it takes tremendous courage of imagination to right an egregious wrong. People born into or assigned the wrong biological gender at birth used to have to live with an identity they didn't recognize as theirs. Today, in many parts of the world they can rectify the situation. Transgender individuals may make the transition at whatever level they choose. This requires medical science and personal determination, and it is always easier if there is a supportive community. But before all else, it requires imagination, the ability to visualize the person they are meant to be.

Interestingly, religious fundamentalists and other narrow-minded individuals often enjoy science fiction when it manifests itself in literature or film but cannot accept the

5. *Lupe's Dream and Other Stories.* Wings Press, 2022.

very real need of transgender people to live their authentic lives. They have neither the imagination nor the compassion necessary to make the leap from fiction to reality.

The foregoing may be an extreme example. But there are many instances in which the first step, the one that unleashes all others, is simply the imagination that enables us to see beyond a fabricated barrier.

What, I wonder, happens to genuine imagination that is exhausted or destroyed before it can fly? It cannot simply evaporate into thin air, leaving no trace of its thwarted energy. Energy cannot be destroyed; it only changes its form. It must wither in frustration, unleashing who knows what in its place. And this can be terribly painful. Something with the potential to be so powerful cannot just vacate the premises without a fight, or without leaving its sad imprint. I think of imagination as a fuel that moves us forward. I shudder to think of what its absence does to our collective capacity for discovery and creativity. And I know many individual instances in which suffocating imagination results in it becoming trapped in the body, causing autoimmune and other problems.

Sometimes imagination—its lack as well as its gift—can best be explained by talking about an actual experience. The Mexican writer Juan Rulfo, who once said, "I believe in silence," came out with a mysterious and compelling novel in 1955. It was called *Pedro Páramo*, and it inhabited an imaginative register not previously explored that profoundly moved a broad readership. This included Gabriel García Márquez, who claimed that reading Rulfo's book enabled him to write his masterpiece, *One Hundred Years of Solitude. Pedro Páramo* is often associated with the magic realism that exemplified many of the books that later came to be known as "the boom" in that continent's literary history, but it actually preceded that period and stands alone as an example of a compelling imagination.

Pedro Páramo is so unique, so rooted in Rulfo's ability to transmit the mystic reality of his childhood, that rendering it in other languages has been difficult. It was first translated into English by Lysander Kemp and published by Grove Press in 1959. Kemp's translation famously excluded whole sentences that seemed opaque or superfluous to him. Put another way, he couldn't deal with the author's imaginative craft. Margaret Sayers Peden, attempting to rectify Kemp's inadequate translation, made one of her own, which was published by the University of Texas Press at Austin in 2002. She overcompensated for Kemp's baffling omissions by adding words to Rulfo's stark prose, thus erring in the opposite direction. Finally, in 2023, Grove reissued *Pedro Páramo*, this time in Douglas J. Weatherford's excellent translation, the one that has done the most justice to Rulfo's original. This story shows that imagination can burst onto the world scene and then be diminished in a variety of ways if those charged with mirroring it aren't up to the task. Capturing another's imagination is clearly more difficult than running with one's own.

Imagination can be about time and space, altering both when necessary. It doesn't doubt itself. It hatches an idea or a vision and then grabs it by both hands, never letting go. It is impetuous and resilient and can change the world.

Fascism Remix

OMINOUSLY FOR ME, although less relevant to the subject, fascism began to gain traction in Europe around the year of my birth, 1936. I'm talking about both fascism and neo-fascist models of governance, the brutal top-down ideology that has led to so much death and destruction. Back then, such tendencies were seen as aberrations by anyone who understood political forces, cared for humanity, and advocated for justice and peace. I've always been curious about what the world was like when my life began: what people were thinking, feeling, doing. But fascist tendencies have existed from the earliest times: in Rome and Imperial China as just two examples.

Fascist parties claiming the name began forming across Europe in the early 1920s. The first was the National Fascist Party, founded in Italy in 1922; the right-wing populist Benito Mussolini launched the movement in response to his country's profound economic crisis and an uptick in social tendencies he saw as hedonist or immoral. Not long afterwards, Hitler organized the National Socialist German Workers' Party, better known as the Nazis. It attempted to erase the existence of an entire people, first curtailing the civil rights of Jews and then sending them to concentration camps where it massively and scientifically organized their wholesale murder. Hitler's alliance with Mussolini made them allies in the Second World War, the conflagration that brought fascism to the shocked attention of the wider world. Japan then joined the axis, opening an additional fighting front in the East.

Although the Second World War demonstrated what fascism was capable of and Hitler especially put an extreme face to mid-twentieth-century fascism, he didn't invent the ideology. Modern-day European fascism originated in the previous century, in opposition to the fear inspired by early social revolutions that put ideas of equality on the table, and it appeared in texts by writers from France and Austria as well as Germany and Italy. These included works by political theorists such as Theodor Fritsch, Paul Anton de Lagarde, Julius Langbehn, Jörg Lanz von Liebenfels, Joseph de Maistre, Charles Maurras, and Georges Sorel; scientists and philosophers such as Johann Gottlieb Fichte, Giovanni Gentile, Gustave Le Bon, Friedrich Nietzsche, Vilfredo Pareto, Karl Vogt, and Ernst Haeckel; historians and social thinkers such as Joseph-Arthur de Gobineau, Hippolyte Taine, and Heinrich von Treitschke; artists, writers, and journalists such as Gabriele D'Annunzio, Richard Wagner, Édouard Drumont, Maurice Barrès, Guido von List, T. S. Eliot, and Ezra Pound; and conservative politicians such as Otto Böckel and Adolf Stoecker. Except for Nietzsche, Wagner, Eliot, and Pound, these names may not be familiar to anyone but scholars of that period in Western history. But research shows us that there were plenty of people in all fields who espoused some form of fascist ideology.

Not all punitive ideologies meet the standard of full-fledged fascism, but crossover is common, and the more traditional right-wing movements often adopt fascist policies or go to fascist extremes. Although it's important to distinguish the differences between these regimes, the danger of slipping into full-fledged fascism is always present.

Racism is often central to the fascist or neo-fascist ideology. In October 2023, for example, Donald Trump declared that undocumented workers were "poisoning the blood of our country," a claim reminiscent of Hitler's white supremacy and racial hatred. There is a disdain for the poor and marginalized in such an ideology as well as for free-thinking writers and artists, and for anyone who works for real justice. A blame-the-victim mentality is always part of the equation. "Might makes right" is the preferred methodology, and scapegoating its most useful tactic. Religions with strong hierarchical structures make for natural collaborators. Fascists understand the importance of culture and restrict or manipulate it in different ways. They disdain difference and oppose identity politics as well as any measure that encourages the inclusivity of marginalized groups. The neo-fascist agenda favors corporations and wants to reduce government to its minimum expression.

I am interested here in the present-day worldwide increase of brutal dictatorships under any name: how they justify themselves and why, despite the warnings of history, people of diverse backgrounds willingly vote them into office. A recent case in point is Javier Milei, the newly elected president of Argentina. The moment he assumed office, he dissolved that country's ministries of Culture and of Women, Gender and Diversity, as well as merging those of Energy, Mining, and Communications into a single Ministry of Infrastructure. He privatized all major industry, devalued the peso, and promised prison sentences to anyone protesting his edicts, leaving no doubt as to the direction of his government.

We see this sort of authoritarian behavior in the leaders of all charismatic cults who control large groups of followers and employ fascistic methods to keep their believers in line. In 1978, Jim Jones, the California preacher who founded the People's Temple, lured more than a thousand men, women, and children to an agricultural commune in Guyana he named Jonestown and induced them to drink Kool-Aid laced with cyanide, causing a massive massacre passing itself off as suicide. Nine hundred people died, a third of them under the age of seventeen. Jones is an extreme example. Most cult leaders only steal their followers' life savings, break up their families, and bed their women. But all such experiences demonstrate the powerful draw that crazed minds can exert over willing converts. When voting majorities of entire nations succumb to the rhetoric, we must search for more complex answers.

Despite their prominence in European thought, fascist ideas gained large numbers of adepts only when perceived economic threats increased their appeal to members of certain social groups. In 1928, before the onset of the Great Depression, Hitler received less than three percent of the vote. After 1930, far more voters, many of them middle- and lower-middle-class people who feared losing what they still had, joined the Nazi party. Leadership disproportionately reflected the economic elites and other influential groups such as university professors, high school teachers, high-level civil servants, former military officers, doctors, lawyers, businessmen, and large landowners—all individuals whose opinions are taken seriously and who tend to influence others. In both Germany and Italy, people from the countryside and small towns were more likely to be lured to the rank and file of fascist parties than their more sophisticated counterparts in urban areas. This tendency can be seen in the United States as well, where rural areas are almost always more conservative and right-wing than cities.

The horror of the Holocaust in which the Nazis systematically exterminated six million Jews, three million Slavs, four hundred thousand Roma, and tens of thousands of homosexuals and others considered undesirable in camps designed for that purpose drew broad repudiation from every person with humanistic values. This wasn't killing in the heat of battle or desperation of self-defense. It was the cold, calculated, and scientifically organized murder of those presumed inferior or guilty of tainting an idealized national image.

Had it not been for the counteroffensive of the Soviet Union—a nation that sacrificed twenty-seven million of its citizens—the brave resistance of England, France, the Netherlands, Denmark, and other European countries, and the late but important entrance into the war by the United States, a whole continent might have fallen prey to Hitler's mad grab for power.

And this is precisely my first point: the world of my youth considered Hitler a madman, an aberration to be dealt with and defeated, not a prophet or precursor of times to come. After the war, the Charter of the International Military Tribunal famously brought to trial in Nuremberg twenty-one of the most important surviving leaders of Nazi Germany as well as of six German fascist organizations. The purpose of the trial was not only to convict the defendants but also to assemble irrefutable evidence of Nazi war crimes, offer a history lesson to the defeated Germans, and delegitimize that country's criminal elite.

In subsequent decades, hunting for Nazis hiding under other names became a cause to which Jews throughout the world devoted themselves. In the early 1960s, Adolf Eichmann's highly publicized trial held global attention. Hannah Arendt, who attended it, coined the phrase "the banality of evil," by which she meant that even apparently ordinary people who are "neither perverted nor sadistic" but "terribly and terrifyingly normal" have within them the capacity to commit such crimes. Eichmann insisted that he had only followed orders, something demanded of foot soldiers in any military structure. Following orders is often the excuse, the way participants try to avoid personal accountability. According to Arendt, Eichmann had committed evil acts without being evil. To this day, the banality-of-evil thesis provokes energetic discussion. Many thinkers cannot accept the fact that an otherwise "normal" individual would subscribe to such a heinous philosophy or be capable of committing such heinous acts.

The post-war world's mantra was: "Never again." Photographs of skeletal corpses and emaciated survivors emerged. Testimonies shamed those who claimed not to have known what was going on and stunned the sensibilities of people everywhere. From politicians to ordinary folk, most vowed to do whatever they could to make sure that the horror of Nazism not be allowed to repeat itself. Those criminals who survived had been punished, and many believed the threat had been eliminated.

This proved to be naive.

Despite solid and abundant historical evidence, including survivors who have told their stories in lurid detail, Holocaust deniers still claim the history of mass Jewish extermination is a lie. And in too many countries subsequent fascistic surges have been permitted to flourish. From 1975 to 1979, Cambodia's Khmer Rouge murdered more than a million of its own people, what we now refer to as the Killing Fields. Pol Pot called himself a communist but was clearly fascist in ideology and action, proving that labels don't always accurately describe what a movement is. In fact, they are often purposefully deceptive.

The following decade, in Latin America, saw the era of "dirty wars." They featured the systematic disappearance of hundreds of thousands. Military dictatorships with their authoritarian structures and strongman tactics carried out mass roundups of members of the opposition, in particular young people, who were plucked from their homes or off the streets and never seen again. This was a new strategy; German concentration camps and the Cambodian Killing Fields had become memorial sites, perpetuating the magnitude and memory of the crimes. Disappearing people left their families without bodies to bury and mourn. It is important to note that the Latin American dictatorships of the 1970s and '80s had the support of the United States. They didn't rise to the definition of fascism in every case but were neo-fascistic in nature and produced horrific genocides. The Nazi genocide hadn't been the first. In modern times alone, the Armenian genocide preceded it in 1915. And it wouldn't be the last.

Mass slaughters in Indonesia, Rwanda, and Bosnia followed, to name just a few. What came to be known as violent sieges of ethnic cleansing exploded quickly, and international response varied depending on whether the victims were black or white, rich or poor. The acts as well as the reactions from the world community were profoundly racist and classist. Although orchestrated by powerful leaders, such fascist episodes didn't necessarily reflect governmental policies.

There has been a great deal of discussion as to what terms should be used to describe states that range from merely authoritarian to those that dissolve all social safeguards or carry out programs of ethnic cleansing. While such distinctions are clearly useful when it comes to organizing against such manifestations, I am most concerned by the ease with which a public that once valued democratic ideals finds it increasingly easy to accept such authoritarianism.

In recent times, despite the warnings of history, fascist or proto-fascist regimes have been voted into power in nations with such diverse histories as Russia, Hungary, the Philippines, Brazil, the Netherlands, Argentina, and the United States. The case of Rodrigo Duterte, who was elected president of the Philippines and served in that office from 2016 to 2022, was particularly interesting; he had a pro-communist background but launched a brutal extra-judicial assault against drug dealers and petty criminals that resulted in the murder of almost seven thousand people.

Despite the intense suffering of the French people during Hitler's occupation, only three generations later France's National Front, now headed by Marine Le Pen, has come frighteningly close to gaining political prominence. She has walked a careful line, expelling her own father from the political party he founded and which she now heads when he repeated the old anti-Semitic lie that the Nazi gas chambers were but "a detail of history." She defends Israel in its war against Palestine. In other words, she has modernized and made more palatable fascism's racist direction.

In the United States, we had four years of Donald Trump, an extreme authoritarian who publicly praises and emulates history's strongmen. His presidency was marked by crimes and coverups in every area. And despite his iron hand having decimated democratic freedoms here at home, disrespecting almost every category of person, exiting international treaties, and putting us at odds with so many of our friends globally, we run the very real risk of another Trump presidency in 2024.

In Nicaragua the Ortega/Murillo regime is clearly neo-fascistic despite its early roots in socialist ideology. It has murdered, imprisoned, or expelled from the country and stripped of their citizenship anyone who opposes it, repressed all journalistic dissent, shuttered the major universities, and ousted more than a thousand non-governmental organizations.

I wasn't surprised by Daniel Ortega's authoritarian turn. After all, he had raped his stepdaughter for nineteen years, while Rosario Murillo sacrificed her daughter's safety and wellbeing to her husband's reputation, an episode largely ignored or swept under the rug by many around the world who call themselves leftists or even feminists. Too many people alleged that his behavior was a personal issue, disconnected from his leadership capacity. I always disagreed. Patriarchy's stranglehold on society still prevents many people from taking seriously crimes committed against women or considering such crimes indicative of broader criminality.

Aside from different flavors of authoritarianism, however, what is fascism? What does it propose and believe? Although its manifestations have been slightly different in different countries, its basic tenets are the following: It is implacably totalitarian. It often posits that there is a "pure" elite that deserves to rule society. This elite is most often male, heterosexual, and supposedly pure-blooded. Survival of the fittest is one of its tenets. People of "inferior" races or identities are belittled, ridiculed, excluded from power, or eliminated. Not all fascists believe in biological racism, but racism of one sort or another is frequently a part of the fascist program. Fascism doesn't invariably lead to genocide, but it has on many occasions and the risk is always there.

Fascists pick on one or more groups and target them mercilessly. Carefully prepared propaganda blames these groups for society's problems. In Germany they were the Jews, those on the political left, and the Roma. Homosexuals and the disabled were targeted because they were seen as polluting the gene pool. Today's scapegoats are frequently

Muslims, immigrants who supposedly take the jobs that nationals need, and people whom the fascists consider of dubious moral standards, claim are bad examples and don't deserve to exist.

Croatian fascists preached the racial inferiority of Serbs and Jews. South Africa's apartheid regime was fascistic and, although it fell short of spawning concentration camps and ovens, its policies induced death in Black townships and ghettos by keeping people impoverished and limiting their mobility and other aspects of social wellbeing. Those who resisted were jailed or murdered.

Tragically, victims of fascism often turn around and use neo-fascistic methods against others. This may be likened to victims of domestic abuse who, if they cannot come to terms with what they've suffered, often go on to victimize others. For the past seventy-five years Israel, claiming a special status because of the mid-twentieth-century Holocaust and a fundamentalist interpretation of Biblical prophecy, invades and occupies Palestinian lands that have housed its Arab sisters and brothers for centuries. Israel's anti-Palestinian laws, illegal settlements, occupation of Palestinian territories, and criminal attacks constitute decades of genocidal policy.

Elsewhere in Europe, as well as in the Middle East, Latin America, and here in the United States, a variety of fascist movements have exhibited cruel racist tendencies. The Ku Klux Klan is an ongoing example of an organization that launches racist attacks against individuals and groups: African Americans and other people of color, Jews, and those espousing liberal ideas. Burning crosses, bombing Sunday school children, lynching Black men, and the entirety of Jim Crow culture are shameful and still largely unexamined parts of our history. We tend to think of the KKK as something of the past, an outdated organization operating primarily in the post-Civil War south. But, although it was founded by ex-Confederate soldiers after the

Civil War, it flourishes to this day, marching legally in northern as well as southern states. And it is not the only fascist movement in our midst. There are many other white supremacist groups, including those who proudly describe themselves as neo-Nazis.

Fascism is opposed to any political position that favors equality: free elections, parliamentary democracy, or equal opportunity for various social groups. This is why it is virulently against Marxists of every stripe, from communists to democratic socialists. This is why it excludes those who don't adopt the traditional binary culture. This is why it fights liberalism and other political ideas that favor egalitarian solutions to problems of class, race, and gender. Fascism promotes conservative economic programs that privilege the wealthy at the expense of the middle and working classes. Corporatism—the organization of industry, agriculture, the professions, and the arts into state- or management-controlled corporations—strips working people of their rights and places power squarely in the hands of a ruling elite.

Fascism and neo-fascism are militaristic in the extreme, demanding unquestioned obedience to authority, discipline, and physical strength. In this, they employ the trappings and actions typical of military organizations, create paramilitary groups such as survivalists, militias, and vigilantes, and encourage regimental marching and the Roman salute. For fascists, the party and state must have a single strong leader wielding absolute power. Youth is glorified but primarily male youth; young men are trained to be entitled and all-powerful, while young women are conditioned to serve their male counterparts and bear them many children.

Extreme nationalism is one of the principal components of fascism. Citizens are encouraged to express a blind pride in country, equal only to their allegiance to God and the nuclear family. Loyalty and patriotism are put forth as important attributes. What patriotism means in any given context is never examined, much less questioned. We in the United States know how patriotism was perverted following September 11, 2001; little attempt was made to understand the policies that led to the attacks, examine the frustration and rage of the attackers, or encourage a national conversation that might have explored the forces at play and lessened the potential for future incidents. Instead, the government's response was superficial and racist and provoked untold crimes against Arabs, anyone presumed to be from the Middle East, and Sikhs.

Education—or a highly controlled version of it—is important in creating and sustaining the fascist mindset. According to the Nazi writer Herman Klaus, the teacher "is not just an instructor and transmitter of knowledge.... He is a soldier, serving on the cultural and political front." The aim of Nazi education was not to encourage students to ask questions or think more deeply but to stir them to a fever pitch and get them to wage war against those they were taught to see as their enemies.

Under fascism or neo-fascism, critical thinking is the first to go. We have troubling examples in the US today of the censorship of important literature, school curriculums modified to ignore historic errors and today's identity issues, and history subverted to support the lies that prevent students from learning about past struggles. Textbooks in several southern states have been altered to depict the institution of slavery as beneficial to the slaves, claiming it protected them. Those who defend such egregious positions say they are tired of our history making white people feel guilty for something that wasn't their fault. Right-wing politicians have been campaigning for school board positions for decades, eventually occupying many of them. This has enabled them to institute such changes. Current attacks on critical thinking in our system of public education are suspect and should be vigorously opposed.

Fascism fights what it considers to be decadence—people who refuse the binary paradigm, women's control of their own bodies, positions that don't support the conventional patriarchal family model, groups seen as female or weak, diversity among peoples (racial or gender difference, homosexuality, gender transformation, new ideas), and any other social manifestation that honors authenticity and challenges tradition.

One of fascism's greatest allies has been Christianity, and it relies on an extreme model of that religion to justify its alleged superiority. Catholicism, with its infallible pope and rigid hierarchy, lends itself easily to this role. The theologically conservative Opus Dei accepts the teaching authority of the Church without question and has long been linked to cultlike practices and rightist political ambitions. The Vatican's long history of refusing the most elemental power-sharing to women and laypeople is an important part of the equation. Even the lowly parish priest holds an authority that protects widespread sexual abuse, othering discriminated groups and furthering intolerance.

It would be unfair if we didn't recognize that reformist movements, such as the liberation theology of the second half of the twentieth century, exist as well within Catholicism and other religious configurations. There are those who identify with what the Church has to offer and are attempting to create change from within. But the world's major religions still overwhelmingly stand for domination and control.

Most fascist movements portray themselves as defenders of Christianity and traditional Christian family values, and against atheists and those they consider to be amoral hedonists. This was especially true of the Catholic fascist movements in Poland, Spain, Portugal, France, Austria, Hungary, Croatia, Bolivia, Argentina, Chile, and Brazil. In Romania, Corneliu Zelea Codreanu, who led the main Romanian fascist organization, the Legion of the Archangel Michael, said he wanted to model his life after the crucified Christ of the Orthodox church.

Christian conservatives have long been counted on to support fascist ideas. Between 1930 and 1932, Hitler was empowered by many Protestant voters in rural Prussia, and after 1933 the German Catholic church accommodated itself to the regime. That year, the Vatican, which had previously prohibited Catholic membership in socialist organizations, signed an agreement with Germany that forbade priests to speak out on political matters and even gave Hitler a say in naming bishops. Pope Pius XI is now broadly known to have had fascist leanings and to have remained silent in the face of even the most egregious of Hitler's policies.

Fascists tend to rely on mainstream philosophies and distort them to meet their needs. They embrace their own brand of spirituality, which gives them a convenient place to hide their criminality. Many Nazi leaders were vegetarians and exuded their love of domestic animals even as they meticulously organized machinery that murdered millions of human beings.

State violence is one of fascism's most powerful weapons. General Miguel Primo de Rivera, founder of the Spanish Falange, famously said that "no other argument is admissible than that of fists and pistols when justice or the Fatherland is attacked." Mussolini sent his Black Shirts to assault socialist organizers throughout Italy, putting many leftists in prison. Hitler's storm troopers served a similar function in Germany. Kristallnacht, or the night of broken glass, the invasion and destruction of Jewish synagogues and businesses, took place November 9, 1938. It was a massive, coordinated attack aimed at reducing Jews to a group exempt from state protection.

What attracts so many millions of people to neo-fascist ideas? Many may be ignorant of what the ideology really means and get hooked through their own lack of political sophistication. Others, perceiving personal benefit, betray causes for which they once claimed to stand. Fascist crimes have sometimes been omitted or erased from history books and school curriculums, and the idea of a strong man capable of fixing all problems can be very seductive to those suffering economic injustice, or to those who perceive that their problems are caused by immigrants or other groups. But there are many who know what fascism is and the crimes it has committed, and who still support it without question. With fascism now a part of the mainstream discourse, it may seem more acceptable. Memory erasure plays an important role here; if we aren't taught about the crimes of fascism, it is all too easy to repeat them.

Lies are also useful weapons in the fascist arsenal. Fascist leaders tend to possess a commanding presence and loud voice. They may repeat the lies that bolster their position so often and with such insistence that they are perceived as truth. This may involve the distortion of scientific data or the scapegoating of vulnerable populations. Hitler pushed the idea that Jews were financially devious, biologically impure, and polluted the Aryan gene pool. In every culture where fascism has flourished, people have been urged to believe things that went against their better instincts and interests as well as against their own experience.

Donald Trump's presidential candidacies offer many clues to how easy it is to convince even those who, if asked if they support this or that fascist position, might say they don't. They are seduced by the image, the figure of strength. Trump's lies have been legion and insistently repeated, leading up to the most flagrant of them all: that he won the 2020 election. "Stop the steal" became a slogan that continues to rally millions.

Both during his first campaign and while in office, Trump consistently maligned women and immigrants, yet many in both groups have voted for him. He openly admires and calls his good friends the world's most prominent dictators, such as North Korea's Kim Jong Un and Russia's Vladimir Putin. During his first campaign, he claimed he could go out and shoot someone on New York's Fifth Avenue and get away with it, and that didn't seem to faze a significant portion of the electorate. A recording was revealed on which he could be heard boasting about getting away with assaulting women, and even that made no difference. At one of his campaign appearances, he openly ridiculed a man with disabilities. Yet none of these remarks or actions proved sufficient to defeat him at the polls. It may be that such open expression of disdain reflects what many people feel but are afraid to admit. They may respond positively to a politician who legitimizes their own insecurities and prejudices.

Trump's presidency was characterized by his promise to designate funds to build a wall between Mexico and the United States, in order to prevent undocumented refugees from entering the country. He also promised to suspend immigration from Muslim-majority countries because of the presumed threat of terrorism, and to deport all eleven million undocumented immigrants, the great majority from Latin America. This created a culture of hate and fear against "the other." During the four years of Trump's presidency, reported hate crimes directed at minorities, especially Hispanics, Muslims, and Jews, increased significantly.

Centuries of patriarchal values have conditioned us to admire the strong man, even the bully. When do these characteristics come together to create a fascist? A boy may mistreat his classmates and we say: *Boys will be boys.* A father or husband may display authoritarian tendencies and we shrug it off as *Men will be men.* A military, political, or religious leader takes command, and we are grateful for his strong leadership. We tend not to question authority when we believe it protects us. For individuals or movements to become truly fascist, they must repress whole populations or lead millions to their death. By that time, removing the criminal from power generally requires a coup.

Militarism is insidious. It has even betrayed movements based on a genuine desire for equality. Left-wing organizations have too often proven themselves incapable of engaging in real gender equality because they refused to relinquish male control and their top-down structures avoided entertaining a change that would threaten that. The excuse for not permitting such an analysis has most often been the need for unity. *We must stick together in the face of enemy attack*, the leaders plead, vowing that problems of gender disparity and other inequalities will be addressed once total victory is achieved. My experience has shown me that time never comes.

We need to understand the insidious path from language to action. A racist joke or offhand remark may seem inoffensive, nothing but a figure of speech or cultural idiosyncrasy. We may even join in the laughter, afraid to appear out of step with others. This is a slippery slope. I remember picking my youngest daughter up at her daycare center in Cuba one afternoon and my shock as I heard her teacher telling all the kids with "good hair" to line up over here, those with "bad hair" over there. She was readying her small charges to go home, afro pic in one hand, comb in the other. When I complained, I was told, "You don't understand, that's just how we describe hair here." Such declarations perpetuate racist stereotyping which in turn can lead to hate crimes. The school bully, if not stopped, too often grows up to be the arrogant agent of more serious conduct. We overlook seemingly unimportant racist manifestations at our peril.

I came of age in a world that pitted communism (the Soviet Union and its eastern European satellites, China, Vietnam, and Cuba) against an increasingly decadent model of predatory capitalism. Socialist countries were in the minority, but their existence at least provided a balance of sorts. I admired communism's promises of workers owning the means of their production and equal rights for everyone. And I saw ample evidence of an ideology that did in fact improve lives during the eleven years I lived in Cuba. The Soviet Union and China elevated millions of their citizens out of poverty and met their basic needs with work, education, and universal healthcare. But I believe that one of the things that prevented these socialist experiments from making a real analysis of the way power operates in their societies was the fear of relinquishing control. This made it impossible for them to examine the roots of inequality or refine what true revolution might mean.

And then there were the hidden crimes committed in some of the socialist countries. Knowledge of sieges of terror emerged slowly and were at first treated as anomalies or anti-communist lies. I still remember Cuba's leadership claiming, in 1975, that the mass murder of one-third of Cambodia's population by the Khmer Rouge was a fabrication perpetrated by Western journalists. When I learned the horrific truth, that was the moment I stopped taking every revolutionary claim at face value. I still consider myself a socialist but one who questions everything.

Gradually, defenders of the socialist model have had to contend with the reality of such crimes: Stalin's gulag, China's brutal Cultural Revolution, Ceausescu's reign of terror in Romania. Following the 1989–1990 collapse of what we now refer to as "real communism," deficiencies in several other so-called communist or socialist systems became too obvious to ignore. I can no longer support the Maduro regime in Venezuela, for example, which as of this writing has forced eight million people into exile.

China's one-child policy, as well as the policies enacted in countries that reward women who give birth to numerous children, are examples of woman abuse, if not frankly measures of fascistic control. Even in so-called democracies, the patriarchal and religiously inspired tendency to control women's reproductive rights is fascistic in essence. I find it deeply concerning that today, even as so many countries in the world are legalizing abortion, the United States is limiting a woman's right to decide whether she will have children, or how many.

When governments built on egalitarian principles show themselves to be less than what they claim, or go bad from greed and corruption, the vacuums they leave behind frequently usher in an authoritarian alternative. People tend to favor a "strong hand" capable of "cleaning up" bad governance. We saw this at the city level in New York, where Mayor Rudolf Giuliani's strongman methods between 1994 and 2001 did in fact reduce crime—for the white elites, rather than people of color and the poor. They also limited individual freedoms and created greater inequality for marginalized groups.

Nationalism is the extreme edge of pride in one's heritage and gives people something to feel good about. In many instances, these "solutions" descend into full-fledged fascism. Would-be leaders who promise to "take care of the problem" are too often power-crazed loners who dispense with thoughtful discussion and democratic safeguards. Religion or other dogma may be employed to provide a spiritual justification. This was certainly the case here in the United States with Donald Trump, who promised to deal with the threat to white ruling-class privilege that it experienced under the eight years of Barack Obama's presidency.

I am deeply troubled by the ease with which so many in my own country and abroad today accept a neo-fascist ideology as necessary or even desirable. In recent years, many things once considered unacceptable have gained a measure of acceptance. Nuclear power is one of these, the use of torture in war another.

Fascism is not simply another political choice, such as parliamentary democracy, state capitalism, or socialism. Advanced capitalism has shown itself to be grossly unfair to most people, but there is room for opposition and rule of law. Fascism is something else. It is barbarism elevated by the latest in technological advances. Allowing it to prosper will invariably mean death and destruction from which it may be impossible for us to escape. Along with global warming and the prevalence of war, I believe it is a major threat to life on earth.

What those who support fascism forget is that extreme authoritarianism not only attacks what may make them uncomfortable but can just as easily eliminate what makes them free.

Discipline, the Forgotten Art

In a recent conversation with my daughter Sarah about a new health issue in my life that requires the discipline of following a strict low-salt, low-fat, low-carbohydrate diet, she said: "We all learned discipline in Cuba, so I know you'll succeed."

It's true that our eleven years in Cuba taught us to be disciplined about many things—learning as much as possible about our jobs in order to increase both quality and productivity, engaging in revolutionary emulation rather than capitalist-style competition, getting up before dawn to join other volunteers harvesting potatoes or some other crop (and participating in such voluntary work even when we were tired), making sure not to waste our scant food rations, and contributing in other ways to the enormous effort required to change society for the better. It was also one of the things that sustained us as we stood for hours beneath a blazing sun in Havana's Revolution Square listening to

Fidel give an unparalleled lesson in history or economics. Interest, passion, and admiration for the man's brilliant mind were key, yet it still took discipline to remain attentive in such conditions.

But the truth is, although I increased my capacity for discipline in Cuba, I learned the practice years earlier when I lived among a group of abstract expressionist artists in New York.

I was an aspiring young poet, recently arrived in the metropolis from the small southwestern city where I'd grown up. I landed in an outsider community of older, more experienced creative people with many preconceived notions about how one learns the skills of an unconventional trade. When I complained to the painter Milton Resnick that I was having a hard time concentrating on my incipient writing process, he told me discipline was the key: "Develop the habit of working for a specific period each day," he said, "even if you must sit before a blank page. Eventually you'll write something on it."

It took me a while to realize that he wasn't talking about an arbitrary exercise but about weaving this new modality into the texture of my life, incorporating it into my daily practice, making it a part of who I am. All the artists I knew back then put their work before anything else and still struggled to find time for it. We played only when the day was done, and our play often included visiting one another's studios to appreciate or critique a new painting or read a poem to friends in the cool summer embrace of the grass at Washington Square Park.

It also gradually became clear to me that Resnick wasn't going to hound me with his advice or ask for updates. He'd answered my question and that was enough. The rest was up to me. I would learn what it takes to be a writer, or I wouldn't. Urging someone to be disciplined is a lost cause. It's something you must take upon yourself, with all the energy of your deepest need and a sense of the responsibility that life's major challenges demand.

Internalizing Resnick's simple exercise not only enabled me to set aside a consistent amount of time each day devoted to my writing but, just as important, taught me to honor that craft by demanding a space in which to develop it. I wasn't always able to have the proverbial room of my own. Sometimes it was only a writing surface: in New York an old oak rolltop desk purchased at a Salvation Army store for seven dollars, in Cuba a glitzy mirror- and goldleaf-faced dressing table in the bedroom I shared with my partner at the time. (The apartment our family was allotted, like so many others, was furnished with what had been salvaged from the mansions of the bourgeoisie who'd fled the island with the revolutionary takeover.) As I progressed in life, what had often been a makeshift desk became a room. And no matter what the demands of motherhood or working wifehood, the time I spent in that room became more precious and inviolate. Those disciplines of time and space wove together to help me protect a practice that continues to be central to who I am. If it did anything, my experience in Cuba encouraged me to extend what had been a very personal routine to one that could also be collective: carrying my weight while working with others to achieve a common goal.

And that early teaching has helped me in many other areas of my life. In the late 1970s, while living in Cuba, I wanted to learn photography. I apprenticed to a fine Cuban photographer, Ramón Martínez Grandal, and learned at his side. We had the most makeshift of darkrooms, with running water only sporadically, and had to mix our own chemicals and beg friends who visited from the United States for film and photographic paper. What we lacked in material products we made up for with discipline—the discipline born of passion. In subsequent years, when I was able to have better darkrooms and easier access to materials, that same discipline translated into spending ten- or twelve-hour stretches developing and printing my work. I frequently didn't even realize how long I'd been in the darkroom.

Doing and making involve training the mind and the body, learning new techniques and freeing expressive potential. Process lives in cellular memory as well as in bone and muscle mass. Just as weightlifters work in periodic increments to add a few pounds to their benching ability or runners add a mile or two to their daily workout, those in the arts increase our ability by developing patience, giving ourselves time to dream, paying attention and studying the work of others, honing our craft, refining our talent, making important connections, and evolving new ways of engaging with both process and product.

Acquiring a healthy balance is also important. There is this basic discipline I've described, and there is also discipline taken to an extreme. Sometimes it can be hard to tell the difference.

Still, it can be difficult to keep working steadily and with discipline when society doesn't reward us for doing so. Showing up may be 95% of what's required, but even the most steadfast workers need to feel their labor is appreciated and that they will reap some benefits along the way. This is especially true for the artist, writer, scientist, musician, or athlete—anyone chasing long-term goals without the structure and security of a nine-to-five job.

It was as a poet that I learned the importance of discipline. I began to understand that it is strategy as well as tactic, the underbelly of all we make and do. We must embrace it unapologetically, with pride, demanding time and the appropriate conditions to be able to see it through. In literature and the visual, performing, and interpretive arts, discipline is a key ingredient. Making art in any genre is frequently an isolated endeavor, which can make it that much more challenging. Writers and artists mostly hone our skills alone, in a self-imposed isolation that must feel right to be endured. Hours, days, months, years of practice are required, in many cases without feedback or recognition. It is frequently in these difficult conditions that we must acquire a lifelong habit of discipline.

Not only writers need this sort of discipline, but those who engage in all the creative genres. For a painter, this is the sort of discipline that links intention, talent, gesture, and brush. For a dancer, it turns the body into a machine capable of defying gravity, expressing the impossible, and creating magic. For an actor, it is what allows one to embody the character on stage rather than simply playing that character. It's what allows a composer to hear every instrument in a large orchestra simultaneously and imagine how they will sound together.

Artists, writers, and other creatives need to develop discipline in the making of our work, as well as in the way we present that work to the public. This may be complicated for those of us who have placed ourselves at the margins of society's conventions. We must be able to prioritize what we do, yet it's important not to put the finished product out there before it's ready. We must decide if we want to live from our art or take a job that can support us and do our creative work afterhours. We must be careful when considering the best venue for publishing and how we want to introduce the work to its target audience. We must resist the temptation to publish too soon or exhibit before the work matures. And we also need to think about what discipline we demand from an editor, publisher, bookseller, or gallery owner, reflecting the same ethical standards we've set for ourselves.

A poetry collection or novel may be turned down dozens of times; most writers accrue an impressive number of rejection slips. Because materials are expensive, it can be even more difficult for a painter or sculptor. Competition is always intense, and getting a gallery is only the first step. Even when a show is scheduled, it doesn't necessarily translate into reviews or sales. When it does, we need to be careful about allowing financial success or an overblown desire for recognition to influence our ongoing practice.

That discipline I learned soon after arriving in New York City is what enables me, as a poet, to take the language employed in everyday speech and turn it into something that translates not only meaning—each word saying precisely what I want it to say—but also originality and emotion to the page. This is no ordinary discipline, but the consistent effort that can produce our best work.

There are experiences in which the panorama is even more complex. For example, employing discipline to rid oneself of an addiction can be tricky. It's important to do away with the compulsion, especially if it is life-threatening. At the same time, the discipline one enlists can itself become an addiction. To be part of a healthy lifestyle, the art of discipline—and it is an art—must be read into the mind/body construct. A variety of options, from Alcoholics Anonymous to expensive inhouse detox treatment programs, all emphasize some form of personal accountability.

Even when one seeks help in overcoming an addiction, I don't believe it is possible to succeed until such time as the desire to quit is compelling. People often speak about "hitting bottom," reaching a point at which it's clear that the alternative is unimaginable if one doesn't seriously change one's behavior.

The mind/body connection works by way of a feedback loop; the way you feel influences the way you think and vice versa. The link between our memory, genes, thoughts, attitudes, and behaviors and our physical abilities has only recently been explored in any detail, and it's still not fully understood. Depending on the addiction we are trying to break and how long it has dominated our life, ridding ourselves of it may require a dramatic break from long-internalized habit. Or it may be better to attack it slowly, in measured increments. In either case, the goal is to replace an unhealthy practice with the discipline that allows us to overcome it.

I was fifteen when I began to smoke cigarettes, probably out of rebellion or in response to peer pressure. Whatever the reason, my body quickly became addicted. Before long I was smoking three packs a day, reaching for my first cigarette while still half asleep and finishing the last just before turning in for the night. By the time I was in my late twenties, I had a constant hacking cough. My son Gregory, even as a young boy, tried everything to get me to stop. I couldn't.

When I brought my youngest, Ana, home from the hospital, I was thirty-two and had been a chain-smoker for seventeen years. She was underweight and delicate. Only a few days into her life, I was sitting cross-legged on my bed nursing and with the proverbial cigarette dangling from my lips. A large wad of ash was balanced precariously and threatened to fall on my baby's pulsing fontanelle. When I happened to look at our reflection in a full-length mirror across the room, the image shocked me into a determination I hadn't experienced before.

That was the last cigarette I smoked.

It's been more than half a century now. The first year was agony, particularly since it included three months underground in the aftermath of Mexico's 1968 Student Movement. Traveling across the immense city, from one hiding place to another, with four young children in tow and constantly evading paramilitary forces and police, quitting smoking seemed like an additional problem I didn't need. Perhaps that also made quitting more imperative to me. My hands shook and I frequently dissolved into tears, but I held to the task at hand. Very gradually my lungs cleared, the worst of my cough disappeared, and the effort became easier. Eventually, being close to smokers and forced to inhale their secondhand fumes was irritating rather than tempting.

I remember the discipline required for me to stop smoking as brutal and all-consuming. Going cold turkey, as they say, may not work for everyone or with all addictions. Drugs such as heroin or opioids require a period of reduced intake so as not to shock the system. But I've often worked to change a bad habit or to develop a good one by exchanging the addiction to the former for an addiction to the latter. If I hadn't been so intent on never smoking another cigarette, I wouldn't have been able to defeat my habit. I had to exchange the addiction to nicotine for an addiction to quitting.

It should be clear by now that what I am talking about is self-discipline, the ability to develop a practice that allows us to excel at what we want to do or make, irrespective of social restrictions or condemnation. This may involve dispensing with established standards. It may break all rules except for the driving need to achieve the ultimate in our chosen field. It is highly controlled, but not by outside forces. If we want to be the best at what we do, discipline is the practice that trains the essence of who we are to always act in our best interests.

Being urged to change our behavior by others rarely works. As a girl and young woman, I tended to overeat. The habit continued for much of my life. Early on, my mother, who was slender and fit, would repeatedly tell me that all I needed was willpower. "Just don't have dessert," she would admonish, as if my extra poundage was something I could rid myself of through discipline. This wasn't my discipline but hers. Eventually I was able to deal with my weight after dealing with the issues that had caused me to overeat. It was only then that I achieved a healthy body.

Discipline imposed from without rarely succeeds in helping us create the consistent practice we are trying to develop. More extreme and devious examples than that exercised by my mother include routines imposed by cults or other controlling institutions, for instance the discipline of silence that certain religious orders impose. The writer Thomas Merton, with whom I corresponded in the 1960s, shared with me his struggle to refrain from speaking and writing, and how he finally felt he had to leave the Trappist order so he would be able to further develop the intellectual exchange that would enable him to advance in his own writing practice.

It can be painful at first to invite discipline into your life, to begin a personal relationship with the practice. But it's only painful because it isn't yet familiar. Once it becomes as natural as breathing, sleeping, or eating, discipline should no longer hurt. It should be deeply satisfying. And there are also those who link discipline to pain. They see the two as equated or at least interrelated. For many writers, the idea that tragedy produces the best work is all too common. I don't embrace that idea. A painful experience may motivate fine art or a brilliant performance in whatever field, but an exuberant experience may as well.

There are of course areas of activity and times of life in which even discipline won't help. My wife and I started going to a climbing gym when I was in my early sixties, she in her late forties. We were anomalies there; most of the others were fit young men and women who treated us with gentle respect and offered helpful pointers. We would go every day after work and practice for a couple of hours. We both advanced quickly and came to love the sport.

But then our daily workout was interrupted. We both got the flu, which meant that we couldn't get to the gym for a couple of weeks. I made a trip right after that, extending my absence to a month. When we finally returned, it was clear we'd lost what skill we'd been able to acquire. And our muscle memory was no longer capable of regaining it. Try as we did, we were unable to bring our levels of ability up to where they'd been before the interruption. Finally, convinced we were stuck, we gave up. It wasn't a lack of discipline so much as the fact that our out-of-shape bodies simply couldn't rebound to their previous capabilities.

Sometimes the challenge to developing discipline faces additional obstacles. For centuries and even today, gender discrimination has worked against women having the conditions needed to prioritize the practice. Women generally face greater problems than most men; those with children face even greater ones. One of my husbands, who wrote occasional poems and articles, occupied the only study in our home, while I had only a corner of our shared bedroom. People of color, the poor, and other marginalized groups often lack the privilege of time and space. Creative people who don't have the money for tools or the leisure to use them are at a dramatic disadvantage.

Discipline today often appears completely out of step with contemporary life. Ours has become a society in which the quick fix rules. Every commercial, every prescription for success, is about how to take a shortcut rather than work slowly but steadily toward a goal.

It's as if we've forgotten the prophetic tale of the tortoise and the hare.

We have become a nation of followers, where political strongmen, religious gurus, supposed experts, and ready-made solutions encourage courses of action in which we don't have to think for ourselves. I'm not talking about exaggerated situations but about the simple matter of doing a thing with the constancy that allows us to master every tool at our disposal, to create a little better each day. This generally requires devoting a significant amount of time to trial and error. Not seeking immediate satisfaction but rather long-term improvement.

Our culture itself often insists on pulling us in a safer direction. It tells us it's important to be accepted, liked, applauded. It measures success in ways that are harmful to our creative instincts. For an artist or writer, this may cause us to pay undue attention to reviews. There is pressure to produce work that is fashionable or sells rather than that which is authentically our own, and this pressure may push us to take shortcuts, keep us from traveling the long slow road to self-discipline. We often find ourselves having to make excuses for, or being forced to defend, the very practice that is most essential to our growth.

Unfortunately, our schools prepare us all too well for such superficiality, with their emphasis on multiple-choice tests as opposed to the longer and deeper route of critical thinking. And now there is also AI which, while useful in many ways, makes it possible for people to claim texts as their own that have been written entirely by a computer. This tendency to follow the easiest road has also produced an uptick in plagiarism. Stealing the work of others used to be fairly easy to detect; now doing so is all but impossible, and we find it in the curriculum vitae of would-be politicians, university professors, and other professionals as well as in the work of an increasing number of students.

Taking shortcuts to avoid the discipline of steady work should not be confused with efficiency. It's only when efficiency undermines discipline that it becomes problematic. Discipline is essential no matter what field we're in, while efficiency is extremely useful and yet another quality we develop through experience and as new inventions and aids enable us to work better and faster. In my lifetime alone, computers have replaced typewriters, spell-check has taken the place of white-out, and online dictionaries have largely relegated to the past those heavy tomes with type too small to read without a magnifying glass.

In a get-there-first-no-matter-what-it-takes environment, developing the slow, steady habit of discipline isn't the norm. Yet in every field we can see how those who cultivate a disciplined approach to their work are able to go deeper, stay longer, produce more authentically, and make the most solid contributions.

It's also important not to confuse discipline with rigidity. The latter can become an impediment rather than an aid. Discipline can only be imposed from within. If it comes from outside, it can be self-defeating.

It should surprise no one familiar with my life that I have been as concerned about discipline in the context of the struggle for social change as I have been as an artist. In the political struggles of the 1960s through the 1980s, we were Davids fighting Goliaths. The enemy had tremendous resources: economic superiority, a sophisticated propaganda machine, expertly fashioned lies and control of the mass media that reproduces them, diplomatic strength, and—when it was required—both covert and overt military might. We had only ourselves and the conviction that in our struggle for a more just world we had right on our side. Discipline was essential if we had any hope of outwitting such a powerful adversary. Guerrilla warfare, in all its modalities, became the norm.

There are many examples of the successes revolutionary discipline made possible in those years. Perhaps the most notable was Vietnam, where a powerful invading army proved no match for small fighting detachments that often remained unseen until they struck and won one battle after another. The Vietnamese rode bicycles while the US invader had tanks. The Viet Cong constructed hundreds of miles of tunnels beneath the enemy's well-provisioned bases, tunnels that housed living quarters, communal dining halls, schools, operating theaters, and more. Those tunnels remained undiscovered until the war's end. Because they were fighting to defend their homeland and believed passionately in what they were doing rather than simply being used as cannon fodder for doctrines they didn't understand, the Vietnamese possessed a discipline that couldn't be matched. This, more than any other factor, made it possible for them to defeat the world's most technologically advanced army.

So, neither a discipline imposed from outside, nor the memorization and rote learning too often found in our schools, but an internal practice developed out of our need to advance in whatever field at a slow and steady pace, can help us craft our best work.

Discipline may be attempted at any time of life, but it is most successfully embraced when the body and mind are young and able to easily adjust to such a rigorous practice. The earlier we start, the better. But whatever our age, discipline is important to advancing in our creativity, changing our lifestyle, addressing social ills, and achieving any long-term goal.

Religion and Social Change

After Cuba's 1959 revolution, religious institutions, primarily Catholic, became centers of opposition to systemic social change. Priests gave counterrevolutionary sermons. Religious schools refused entrance to Afro-Cuban students. Catholic Charities organized Operation Peter Pan, which sent thousands of children to foster parents in the United States, presumably saving them from communism. The Cuban government, in response, restricted all religious practices. Catholic churches and schools were shut down. Santeria and other African rituals were disrespected in their essence while being exploited for their folkloric value to tourism. Sects such as Jehovah's Witnesses were illegalized because their members wouldn't join the military and refused life-saving blood transfusions. Most importantly, no people of any religious faith were allowed to join the Cuban Communist Party because religion was contrary to the Party's Marxist philosophy. Being denied Party membership was serious. It meant being excluded from the front lines of social change at a time of exciting national transformation. Many priests and ministers of other denominations left the country. The government confiscated Church buildings along with other property belonging to a fleeing bourgeoisie. Believers who supported the revolution kept their religious convictions to themselves.

Soon, Pope John XXIII initiated the great social movement that was Vatican II,[1] and what we call liberation theology swept Latin America and much of the developing world. It even took root within working-class neighborhoods in developed countries. It became a prime motivator of social change, such that at the grassroots level liberation theology congregations promoted justice and equality—often putting them in conflict with their own hierarchies. Eventually the hierarchies won out, the institution proving itself stronger than its progressive outliers. Priests who espoused liberation theology were punished, disempowered, often expelled from their parishes.

Nevertheless, many young people throughout Latin America came to social activism through their participation in Christian base communities. This was especially true in Nicaragua, where I lived from the end of 1980 through the beginning of 1984. In the mid-1980s Ernesto Cardenal, the Nicaraguan priest and poet, famously declared that "there is no contradiction between religion and revolution." I didn't question the statement at the time. In fact, I applauded it.

In 1985, the best-selling book *Fidel y la religion* (*Fidel and Religion*) was published in Cuba; it was a condensation of twenty-three hours of conversation held the previous year between Fidel Castro and a Brazilian liberation theology friar named Frei Betto, O.P. In this book, Fidel said that the

1. Also known as the Second Vatican Council, from 1962–1965.

revolution had made mistakes regarding the treatment of religious Cubans, that discrimination against people of faith must end and conditions must be created through which "usage of religion as a counter-revolutionary weapon will be nullified by the confidence and fraternity that will exist among all revolutionaries in our country."[2] I supported this change, in line with my long-held belief that inclusion was always better than exclusion. The idea that no one—women, people of all races, sexual identities, and belief systems—should be left out was an easy one to embrace. When it comes to racial, gender, or sexual identity, it is one that I continue to embrace. I am less certain when it comes to belief.

Fidel assumed responsibility for having excluded believers from Communist Party membership on the grounds that: "What we were demanding was complete adherence to Marxism-Leninism.... It was assumed that anybody who joined the Party would accept the Party's policy and doctrine in all aspects."[3] He told Frei Betto that he now understood that this had been wrong. By 1991, the new policy was implemented, and religious believers could become Party members. In July 1992, the Cuban Constitution was amended to change the country's designation from an atheist state to a secular one, and Article 42 was added, which prohibited discrimination based on religious belief.

The above, very briefly, is the history of one revolution's relationship with religion within the context of what was happening internationally. I tell it here because I lived in Cuba at the time and it's the only socialist country, one specifically calling itself atheist or secular, with which I have

2. Castro, Fidel, and Frei Betto. "Christians and the Communist Party." *Fidel and Religion: Fidel Castro in Conversation with Frei Betto on Marxism and Liberation Theology*. Claremont School of Theology, 1985, p. 192.

3. Ibid.

firsthand experience. I have read histories of other nations that went through radical social change, though, and know they have been similar. An exception may be Vietnam; from the moment that country's revolutionary forces ousted the US military, Buddhists and Catholics were welcomed into the new nation's governing bodies. In the Soviet Union an atheistic state prospered for a time but, as socialism imploded, religion returned with a force that paralleled the revolution's disintegration. China, with its current system of state capitalism, is careful to permit only officially sanctioned religious expressions that do not threaten its control; its crackdown on Tibetan Buddhism and its own Uyghur people is well documented.

Countries with different social systems claim official religious identities ranging from atheist or secular to those of any one of a number of the world's religions. Varying degrees of religious freedom exist in nations that call themselves socialist, capitalist, or democratic, or that are based in other socioeconomic systems. My intention here is not to pit religious freedom against countries for which social equality is central, but to examine religion per se as a phenomenon that exercises hierarchical control, undermines equality, thwarts progress, and stifles critical thought.

Now I want to take a step back in time and revisit an experience I had in 1970. I had recently taken political refuge in Cuba[4] and had been invited to be on the poetry jury of that year's Casa de las Américas literary contest.[5]

4. After participating in Mexico's 1968 student movement, I suffered government repression and was forced to leave the country. Cuba generously received me and my family as it did so many political refugees in those years.

5. Casa de las Américas, Cuba's primary cultural institution, opened its doors a few months after the revolutionary victory of January 1959. Its yearly literary contest continues to attract manuscripts from around

The other four judges were Nicaragua's Ernesto Cardenal, Roque Dalton of El Salvador, Peru's Washington Delgado, and Cuba's Cintio Vitier. As I recall, 192 book manuscripts were submitted that year. We judges had read them all and none had yet struck any of us as a clear winner. Then a last-minute entry arrived. I was the first to read it and immediately felt its power. I handed it off to Roque, who agreed with my assessment.

Roque was concerned, though, with the fact that in his poems the book's author had substituted the name of his country's dictator with that of God, a ruse to make sure the work would be able to make it past the censors and out of the barracks where he was imprisoned without it being confiscated. Roque was afraid that this use of "the Lord's name" might offend Ernesto and Cintio, both devout Catholics. He felt that he and I—the atheists on the panel—would be taking a risk if we were the ones arguing for the book. He suggested we pass it on to Ernesto, hoping the Nicaraguan poet would recognize its impact and recommend it as the winner. Roque's plan worked, and *Diario del cuartel* by Uruguayan Carlos María Gutiérrez was awarded Casa's 1970 poetry prize.

I tell this story for two reasons. First, because it illustrates the contradictions and occasional awkwardness between believers and non-believers at the time. And second, because the whole incident returned to me in a dream all these many years later, leaving me deeply shaken. More than half a century has passed, but I awoke one recent morning disoriented, breathing erratically and ideologically confused. It would be hard to overemphasize the dream's power. My four colleagues are all dead, and I sensed a responsibility to a history I'm not even sure they would

the world in several genres. I have been a judge twice, once in 1970 and again in 2011.

have recognized as still meaningful. I realized that over the past several years I've had to revise my thoughts about religion and social change. And that, given my age, I must write about this revision. Indeed, perhaps it is my age that beckons me to externalize ideas that may be unpopular but that I feel deserve discussion. Perhaps the dream itself acted as a catalyst or detonator.

It is easy to confuse ordinary believers with the ideas they represent. The former surely include good humans, many of whom are friends, selfless people who work for justice and equality. The latter, I am convinced, make up the single most serious impediment to successful social change. Religious fanaticism has carried out a brutal Inquisition that still has repercussions today. It causes genocides, murders doctors who perform abortions, advocates for anti-woman and anti-LGBTQI+ laws, teaches woman's submission to man, causes many young homosexuals to believe they are sick, and inspires guilt and shame in believers, among other travesties. It is out of my conviction of the increasing danger religion poses that I write today.

Many religions operate what they call missions, charitable programs overseas or in inner-city ghettos, through which their more selfless members bring education, health and hygiene, income-generating projects, or other types of aid to disadvantaged and often isolated populations. This is an egregious form of neocolonialism that destroys cultures just as the Christian Crusades did centuries ago. It has been going on for several hundred years and at this point almost seems like a vast game in which the team that ends up with the most members wins. Those involved believe they are performing good deeds, helping the populations among which they stake their claims. But there is always a tradeoff involved. A missionary's main objective is to "save souls," and so they proselytize, attempting to make converts in exchange for the aid given. And these are cookie-cutter plans, prepared without knowledge of the cultures they invade and certainly without asking the people affected what they need or want. It is through such programs that churches spread their influence among more and more people around the world.

One of the most insidious of these projects is the Summer Institute of Linguistics (SIL), an Oklahoma-based evangelical institution. Its mission statement stresses worldwide literacy, but the text it has translated into more than one hundred languages so far is the Christian Bible, and its efforts are clearly aimed at conversion. Its goal is to translate the New Testament into every language on earth. SIL translators are excellent, but the organization is blatant in its disrespect for indigenous cultures. I know of at least one instance in which community elders have refused to work with SIL translators because of a lack of respect for their stories. A group of Wounaan Indians involved in a social anthropology project in Panama noticed that the translators had changed stories that used sexual metaphors or otherwise featured scenes they considered immoral. They rejected this distortion of their traditional culture.

Catholic Charities and a variety of other groups are guilty of similar opportunism. The Church of Jesus Christ of Latter-Day Saints (Mormons) encourages young men to go on overseas missions before marrying and settling down. About 32% of them do so. Young women may also go on missions if they feel so moved. Among the Christian denominations, the American Friends Service Committee (Quakers) alone has the reputation of offering skilled aid (particularly medical) without asking anything in return; during the US American war in Vietnam, it was famous for treating victims on both sides.

In contrast with this worldwide attempt at spreading religious doctrine under the guise of aiding the needy, we might take a look at Cuba's decades-old program of sending doctors, teachers, and other professionals to parts of the world that request its help, often after a calamitous earthquake or hurricane. The Cuban revolution expressly forbids these experts to push an ideological agenda; the example they set is enough. For many years Cuban specialists and aid workers traveled the globe, teaching literacy, doing assembly-line cataract surgeries, cleaning up after a disaster, and even bringing their own food so that the host nation didn't have to spend scarce resources on them. This aid was completely free. In more recent times, many more countries have requested Cuba's help, and Cuba now charges a modest fee.[6]

I understand how faith in the supernatural grew in ancient times. Some such expressions no doubt reflected beliefs that emerged from authentic experiences now lost to obscurity. This may be too simplistic an analysis, but I can imagine people searching for explanations that would enable them to understand the world around them: the change of seasons, violent weather events, birth, death, and other natural phenomena. Some of these quests may eventually have consolidated themselves into what we now call religions. Schisms, almost always political, then fractured them, creating new configurations.

Brilliant thinkers of all eras—Pythagoras, Hypatia of Alexandria, Galileo Galilee, Isaac Newton, Charles Darwin, Marie Curie, Ada Lovelace, Albert Einstein, Rosalind Franklin, Chien-Shiung Wu, and Lise Meitner, to name just a few—rejected religious explanations of any origin and based their findings on observation: Galileo looked through his telescope and reported on what he saw; Darwin made his voyages, taking copious notes on what he found. Karl

6. For a more detailed account of Cuba's overseas aid programs, see my book *Exporting Revolution: Cuba's Global Solidarity* (Duke University Press, 2017).

Marx belonged to this category of observational theorists. His contribution to economic theory is located squarely on the side of science, which by its very definition is always open to further exploration and change.

All these scientists were at first ridiculed for discoveries that broke with accepted assumptions, often religious in nature. They suffered humiliation, marginalization, and worse. Later they were revered for those same discoveries. As serious observation provided more and more complex answers, they discredited the stories religion told.

Yet religion lived on, satisfying a tendency to take solace in tradition, a need for community, a love of pageantry, and as a powerful medium of domination and control. The undeniable power of magical thinking to resist rationality continues, with ever more sophisticated methodologies. It has been weaponized to fight successfully on the front lines of thought.

In the past forty or fifty years, postmodernism has also questioned previously accepted ideas about the ways in which we attempt to understand the world. Distrusting all grand theories, it rejects concepts of rationality, objectivity, and what might be considered universal truths. I believe this has created a vacuum, in which it has been easy for religious dogma to gain traction. All religious believers have to say, in defense of their ideas, is that God gave them the message or instructed them to accept such and such a leader or idea. I think it's important, though, to remember that dogma of any variety—secular as well as spiritual—can lead us astray. It often produces the conspiracy theories that prevent large numbers of people from acting rationally and in their own best interests. We should be wary of any claim to a single immutable truth.

No matter how many believers maintain there is no contradiction between religion and revolution, the truth is religion is posited upon faith in a fictitious power. That faith in someone or something greater than oneself absolves one of personal responsibility for one's behavior and actions. It requires a suspension of belief in science, fosters superstition, curtails curiosity, and exerts an authoritarian control over its adepts. This is contrary to socialist doctrine based on the Marxian science of economics and society. Science-based, it can and should change in differing historical and cultural contexts or as new data becomes available.

Belief in a supernatural power doesn't make one a bad person, but it often prevents one from fully embracing revolutionary social change and the personal responsibility it entails. Nevertheless, we have powerful examples of people of faith who have given their all—including their lives—for justice. The Nicaragua I knew and loved in the early 1980s had many such people: liberation theology priests, Catholic sisters, and young people who were educated at religious schools influenced by the ideas of Vatican II.[7] Before them, there was Father Camilo Torres in Colombia and Bishop Oscar Romero in El Salvador; both men gave their lives from positions of faith as well as out of their absolute commitment to social change. On the opposite side of the spectrum, we can name atheists who sacrificed their lives for their ideals and others incapable of such sacrifice. I can't help wondering if there is some obscure quality apart from belief itself that allows people to live up to their professed values.

In my argument against religion, I won't dwell upon the vast numbers of priests, rabbis, imams, ministers, and gurus who take advantage of their congregants—through a

7. *Christians in the Nicaraguan Revolution* (New Star Books, 1983) focuses on two Christian base communities: one in Managua and the other at Solentiname. The book was also subsequently published in Nicaragua, Venezuela, and Germany.

power disbalance, sexually, psychologically, economically, or in other ways. This sort of corruption can be found in all communities, secular as well as religious. Revolutions themselves are filled with leaders who involve themselves in everything from inappropriate conduct to criminality, from authoritarianism to dictatorship. Mahatma Gandhi, Ho Chi Minh, Nelson Mandela, and Fidel Castro are rare examples of revolutionaries who were true to their convictions in every area of their lives and who were humble enough to admit their mistakes.

Nor will I focus on the many communities where imposing churches are surrounded by hovels inhabited by people in dire poverty who are coerced into giving what little money they have to luxurious buildings and their trappings, a sacrifice considered a requisite for entering the kingdom of God. Although of tremendous concern in my country today, I'm not even going to discuss at any length the separation of church and state inscribed in the United States Constitution that has been under such vicious attack in recent years.[8] Rather, I want to concentrate on religious belief in and of itself: a Petri dish of deceit.

One cannot revere and follow God or one of his self-proclaimed prophets while at the same time professing an

8. Although our nation was founded on the principle of separation of church and state, this principle has been eroded in recent years. Presidents Reagan and George W. Bush went farther than their predecessors in privileging so-called Christian values. Donald Trump installed three justices on a Supreme Court that has taken this shift to dangerous judgments, undoing a woman's right to choose and other long-settled law. In 2022, the conservative majority of the Court chipped away at the wall separating church and state in a series of rulings, eroding American legal traditions intended to prevent government officials from promoting any particular faith. The following year, a religious school in Oklahoma became the first in the nation to be given taxpayer money, a clear violation of the separation of church and state and indicative of where we are headed.

allegiance to the people as the legitimate engine of society. Revolutions have too often substituted top-down party rule for people's power, and that's when they fail. The same can be said of union leadership with regard to the rank-and-file. Authoritarian hierarchies always spell an increased gap between those who have and those who don't, whether we're talking about power, agency, or money. And no matter how religious discourse pretends a "church of the poor," its institutional nature implies a hierarchical order. There is simply no way that submission to a "higher being" can be squared with equality. Religious texts are often rich in metaphor. It's when they are read literally that they are problematic.

These extreme beliefs have long governed large groups of people. They become exponentially more dangerous when they shape a nation's political policy, always leading to authoritarianism, often to fascism or war.

I realize where my rejection of religion situates me in a world with billions of believers. And, again, I will say that I sincerely value individuals no matter their beliefs, their actions always speaking louder than their words. But I would urge that we look at the many ways—obvious and subtle—in which absolute adherence to religious belief impedes human progress. It sends us on superstitious detours that separate us from honest inquiry. It ties us to ideas that distract us from struggle and communities that deter us from rational thinking, often offering inadequate do-good solutions in lieu of systemic change. It enmeshes us in magical thinking that creates social confusion. It reduces responsibility for the here and now, replacing it with the rewards of a supposed afterlife. And it trades personal agency for a presumed need for religious doctrine. In short, it has become a weapon in a time when acting responsibly is more important than ever.

I have been asked by people of faith how I—a non-believer—can discern right from wrong. They seem surprised when I argue that it shouldn't require adherence to some fictitious doctrine to make that determination.

In this age of increased isolation, I understand that bodies of belief can offer a much-needed sense of community. Mormons, for example, who subscribe to what I find to be an outlandish series of ideas about history and an afterlife, are famous for their supportive communities. This communal aid, however, comes with serious drawbacks, such as enforcing patriarchy's rigid laws and regulations, relentless proselytization of a belief system that favors absurd dogma over personal agency, female subordination, the stigmatization of diversity, the curtailment of curiosity, and the stifling of critical thought. We need to develop such community comfort outside of religion.

My life experience—what I have seen in different societies, the movements for change in which I've participated, and the clear evidence that religious doctrine is detrimental to profound systemic change—has convinced me that, well-intentioned as it may be at the individual level, religion is bad for life.

Too much death and destruction have been waged in the name of faith. The Conquest, the Crusades, the Salem Witch Trials, Senator Joseph McCarthy's anti-communist campaign, history's many so-called Holy Wars, and Israel's ongoing genocidal attack on Palestine are all products of unchecked religious fervor, among other reasons. They leave us with misplaced shame, blame-the-victim mentalities, book censorship, campaigns against women's and LGBTQI+ rights, and other assaults on our freedoms. Major denominations have split over these issues, demonstrating how stubbornly people will defend their positions. No amount of apology can erase these travesties. The nations with the highest percentages of atheists have more highly educated, better-informed, and freer populations.

Religion should not be confused with what many call secular spirituality: the mystery and wonder of nature, the power of art, our astonishment at the life cycle. And I am not advocating prohibiting religion or punishing those who engage in its practice. This is not about coercion or retribution. What I would like to see is a natural progression out of darkness into light, a modern-day enlightenment.

I can only hope that humanity will reject its fabricated need for dogma and replace it with belief systems that more effectively contribute to our mental, emotional, and physical survival—and to the survival of our planet.

Softer Landings, or How We Celebrate Ourselves

AT MY AGE, ONE NATURALLY TENDS to do a lot of looking back. This may take different forms. I peruse obituaries and think about how some lives seem fully realized while others are spent in frustration and despair. What, if anything, will be written about me? Perhaps this is why I've been thinking lately about how we perform holidays and—more importantly—commemorate individual milestones.

Every culture has its unique rituals and celebrations, many of them connected to ancient seasonal calendars such as the harvest, successful military battles, national independence, or the birth of some founding father or messianic figure. Some evoke significant remembrance, but most have been diluted or commercialized to the point where they bear scant resemblance to their original significance. I believe this disparity increases as we age, poorly told history distorts it, our commodity-oriented society makes the distance between origin and celebration ever greater, and patriarchy and colonialism imprint it with cruel gender and racial discrimination.

In our commemorations of the big holidays, we are forced to waste time, energy, and resources on a kind of watered-down observance and "keeping up with the Joneses" that lead us to focus on the superfluous and unnecessary. Important personal markers are often ignored. Rather than develop rituals that celebrate who we really are, we settle for the hollow distortions that do nothing to enhance our lives. On the contrary, they may denigrate them. Guilt, shame, humiliation, and a sense of failure can affect health and wellbeing. Social expectations that we live in certain ways and are encouraged to indulge in meaningless but costly rituals can produce accumulated anxiety.

In every culture, long lives are marked by a series of important passages, some collective, others individual.

We celebrate birth, then coming of age, marriage, childbearing—all forward-looking moments—followed by those passages that come toward the ends of lives fortunate enough to have endured: retirement from years of work, a slowing-down of the senses as well as of the body, and finally death.

Certain markers are obvious across class, race, and cultural lines. Societies observe them in different ways, and the rituals associated with their passage are carried out according to the culture and socioeconomic possibilities of those celebrating.

Birth, as I say, is the first of these. Naming ceremonies, christenings, and other religious or secular observations often accompany a child into the world. In most cultures the parents choose their child's name, sometimes after a beloved relative who has died or the saint's day on which the child was born, or simply because it appeals to them or is popular at the time. Celebrity tends to make some names popular, and each successive generation sees a proliferation of those responding to the celebrity of certain figures in the worlds of entertainment and sports. This accounts for the many Britneys and Alis among children born over the past several decades in the United States. Religion plays a central role, which is why there are so many Mohameds in the Islamic world, so many Jesuses and Marías in Spanish-speaking countries, so many Moises and Rachels among Jews.

In some cultures, children are allowed to choose their own names when they reach adolescence or early adulthood. In many indigenous tribes, a name is taken that recognizes a particular attribute or skill or celebrates an event that happened at the time of birth. In many societies these days, non-gender-specific names allow for freedom to assume an identity that fits. Now that we are beginning to understand that some people may not identify with their biological bodies or may feel ambivalent about the gender they were assigned at birth, androgenous names may provide a welcome freedom of choice. Such names feel more authentic to me, especially today when we are beginning to respect individuality beyond a purely binary construct and recognize the needs of gay and transgender people.

For Jewish boys, a bris or ritual circumcision is traditional. Eight days after they are born, a mohel (rabbi or other religious figure) performs the small operation. Tragically, a circumcised penis denounced many male Jewish children during the Holocaust and led to more than a few deaths. For years, non-Jewish boys have also been circumcised, but by a doctor rather than a rabbi. More recently, the medical profession considers the operation unnecessary, even unhealthful. Customs change with the times.

In many places, among them Jamaica, the placenta and umbilical cord of a newborn are saved and buried, the spot then marked by planting a tree. In El Salvador, country people believe they will eventually return to the place where their umbilical cords are interred, the piece itself calling them back. In Mexico, midwives place a cut onion on the belly of a woman to hurry along a delayed labor. In Bihar, India, if a woman's labor is not progressing rapidly enough, she is encouraged to drink a glass of water in which her mother-in-law has dipped her toe. While some birth rituals have explicable origins, there is no accounting for the origins of others. Unfortunately, I think semiotic, symbolic, or thoroughly commercialized rituals are replacing those that embody real meaning.

While male initiation rites often feature pleasure, the courageous withstanding of pain, or a test of power, women are subjected to more humiliating and damaging rituals. From before birth, they are trained to be submissive and to put the needs of men above their own; in some cultures they are forced to submit to operations that will reduce their sexual pleasure and damage their health. In many parts of the world, female genital mutilation (or FGM) is traditional. It is still legal in some countries of Africa, Asia, and the Middle East, along with their respective diasporas. As of 2023, UNICEF estimates that at least 200 million girls in thirty-one countries have been subjected to female genital mutilation. The removal of the clitoris and parts of the vulva leaves young women unable to enjoy sexual intercourse and causes health problems that will accompany them throughout their lives. Laws have been passed prohibiting the procedure, but it continues—often performed in secret and with a dirty knife. Interestingly and perhaps ironically, male circumcision is performed by a man on a male child while genital cutting is most often performed by women upon those of their own gender. We inflict the pain upon our own kind.

Our next life event is coming of age, observed, among other examples, by bar mitsvah or bat mitsvah for Jews, Christian first communion, or Shiite Islam's taklif ritual marking puberty (fifteen for boys and a surprisingly young nine for girls), accompanied by such requirements as study, fasting, and modest dress, the latter most rigorously demanded of the female of our species. Perhaps one of the most extreme examples of using the life of a child to fortify religious doctrine is the Tibetan Buddhist practice of identifying a boy as young as four or five to be the next Dalai Lama. The child is taken from his family, sometimes against its wishes, and introduced into a lifelong process that entails tremendous rigor and sacrifice disguised as honor and privilege.

Most religions require periods of study to prepare the celebrant for such passage into adulthood. Each belief system marks these changes in a unique way. And there are secular customs as well. For example, in many Western traditions it is common for a father to take his son to a prostitute to initiate him into adulthood, symbolically and experientially "making him a man." In the act itself he is teaching the next generation of males that it is alright to use women, thus encouraging society's double standard. Traditionally, among the upper classes in western European countries, young girls in their late teens are presented to society in lavish events, the preparation for and execution of which can cost extraordinary amounts of money.

Among the Amish people of the northeastern United States, both boys and girls between the ages of sixteen and twenty-one are encouraged to experience something called Rumspringa, a period in which the young person may wear modern clothing, use otherwise prohibited technological devices, drink alcohol, and experience courtship with the opposite sex (I know of no such provisions for gay youth).

This period can last as long as two years, after which the young person either chooses the "English" way of life (a strange label having nothing to do with England) or is permanently baptized into the Amish faith.

In Australia, Aboriginal tribes send their boys into the outback for up to six months. Entirely alone, they learn to make their own shelter and survive by finding food and water: a test of their competence and practice in the skills that will serve them throughout their lives. At the age of thirteen, boys of the Sateré-Mawé tribe in Brazil take turns wearing a special glove and allowing the bullet ant to bite them on the hand; the bite is extremely painful, and the boys are initiated into manhood by enduring it some twenty times over a period of several months. Like many other adult initiation rituals, this one requires that the boys not cry out or show weakness in any way. In modern-day urban cultures around the world, being old enough to vote, drive a car, drink alcohol, marry, or join the military all mark a coming of age.

History and geography are filled with age-marking observances that astonish or even shock those outside the culture. In Ethiopia, when they reach a certain age, Hamar boys are expected to engage in a ritual in which they leap over the backs of twenty to forty bulls to demonstrate their manhood. In eastern Africa, young Maasai warriors prove their courage by hunting lions armed with nothing but a spear. Such demonstrations of bravery are common for young men; young women are more often celebrated for their docile or submissive qualities. Few cultures recognize the immense strength and courage required in giving birth, to say nothing of the responsibilities and sacrifices inherent in motherhood: childcare, feeding their families (often as the sole provider), and sublimating their own needs.

Whether observed ritualistically or as a private event, first menstruation is a powerful marker for girls. I can still remember how excited I was by those first drops of blood. It was a Sunday morning and I rushed out of the house to share the news with my closest girlfriends. I had always been told that once I got my period, I would be a woman. Yet menstrual blood is feared in many cultures, considered unclean in some. There are places where during menstruation a girl is forced to live in isolation. The menstrual hut can be a lonely and unsafe place. Evidence of a woman's superpower—her ability to give birth—has always been frightening to men, and many cultures have established ways to punish young girls when they show the first sign of being able to do so.

Throughout Latin America and in US American families of Latinx origin, young girls celebrate womanhood with a party on their fifteenth birthday; a Catholic mass is usually part of the event. White Protestant culture holds a less vibrant replica of such a party a year later: what has come to be known as Sweet Sixteen. Among the very wealthy, such parties can have elaborate themes with complex choreography and cost millions; in working-class or poor families it's a simpler affair. These events mark a coming of age but have been reduced to purely social occasions, without a period of study or any discernible reference to increased experience or responsibility.

Marriage and parenthood follow. Marriage ceremonies around the world are exuberant in their traditions, often costing small fortunes to the parents of the bride, who traditionally foot the bill. Jewish weddings are performed under a huppah, a special canopy that represents the couple's future home, and the bride and groom step on a glass that breaks beneath the force of their feet, symbolizing the fragility of relationships and the need to care for them.

The importance of such values cannot be denied, but perverted standards place undue importance on how much is spent. Indian weddings are particularly elaborate. Even contemporary US marriage ceremonies can be exaggeratedly fancy and cost tens of thousands, with an industry ready to reap the profits. Destination weddings are an important source of revenue for the tourist industry, honeymoons to exotic places an equally profitable market.

Yet contemporary expectations around a great many of these events remain increasingly inaccessible to great portions of the population. In fact, attempting to live up to these expectations can actually create adverse effects for many people, due largely to systemic inequality. In her powerfully convincing book, *Weathering: The Extraordinary Stress of Ordinary Life on the Body in an Unjust Society*,[1] public health researcher Arline T. Geronimus explores the ways in which systemic injustice erodes the health and dramatically shortens the lifespan of marginalized peoples. Through long-term comprehensive studies, she dispels popular assumptions that blame people for their own diseases and disabilities and demonstrates that the overwhelming culprits are poverty, lack of access to good nutrition, safe places to exercise, and adequate healthcare. She proves beyond any doubt that the multiple stresses caused by inequality are the real causes of the grotesque inequities endured by Black, Hispanx, Native American, and poor rural white populations. And she extends this analysis to other highly stressed groups: women, LGBTQI+, transgendered persons, and those who suffer from generational abuse.

Although I certainly agree that an unjust socioeconomic structure, poverty, and discrimination are the main causes of inequality, cultural distortion and the many ways in which society pushes fabricated need also contribute. Early

1. Little Brown, 2023.

death is not primarily the result of violence or drugs but of diseases such as heart conditions, hypertension, cancers, diabetes, and the like. In other words, what kills is societally imposed stress, not how one chooses to live.

As *Weathering* shows us, the ways in which we celebrate all life's important moments and holidays in a commercialized society only add to the burden and especially affect the health of the poor and other marginalized groups. They cannot sit down to lavish celebratory dinners. They experience the humiliation of not being able to give their children the toys that entice from store windows. Their experience is one of being unable to live up to the fabricated standards our societies equate with love and caring. All this can have a devastating effect on their mental as well as physical health.

Hallmark, the longtime commercial curator of prepackaged sentiment, has cards with messages for every occasion. They can be purchased to tell someone you love them, sympathize with a loss, celebrate some special occasion, are sorry for an unintended remark, or just want to be friends. Many other corporate enterprises push the sale of specialized gifts designed to express remembrance and caring. Mother's and Father's days were invented with this in mind. As with Christmas, Rosh Hashanah, Ramadan, and Ganesh Chaturthi, if you "care enough to send the very best" you can buy the emotion rather than having to dwell on the day's meaning and create your own unique way of expressing your feelings. But can we really measure love by the size of a diamond, celebration by a pre-printed message? Maybe in our corrupted culture, but certainly not in any authentic sense.

Middle age, especially in Western cultures, often marks a time that is not so publicly celebrated. The different ways they are spoken about describe the gender difference: "midlife crisis" for men and "change of life" for women. The males of our species may suddenly feel they haven't achieved their dreams or don't have everything they've hoped to accomplish and, if they have the resources, will go on a rampage that involves buying a motorcycle, boat, or some other expensive toy. Not uncommonly they will leave a wife of many years for a younger woman.

For women, menopause, or the cessation of menstruation, is never marked by celebration. On the contrary, it is seen as the moment when a woman's life ceases to be useful and she quite literally becomes expendable. Looking at these very different experiences, and at society's response to them, reads like a road map of gender. We tend to laugh off the male transition—men will be men, after all—while women mostly bear their change in silent discomfort; we give them pills to placate their symptoms, and they are expected to muddle through. In recent years, this hormone-replacement therapy has been proven to cause other ills, such as certain types of cancer, but it continues to be prescribed. And many women, not surprisingly, would rather eliminate hot flashes and mood swings even if it means risking cancer.

And finally, there is retirement for those men and women who have lived professional lives. This is a moment that is almost always ritually observed but has an aura of "good riddance" rather than of real celebration: the now superfluous old person is dispensed with to make room for a younger, more vibrant replacement. There may be the proverbial retirement party, usually involving some version of the gold watch. But retirement is almost always considered an end, not a beginning. What comes next belongs to that vague time we call old age, rarely seen as a period capable of producing anything worthwhile.

With the retirement ritual, aging adults who have spent lifetimes in their chosen professions, loyal to companies that have exploited them shamelessly, or who have simply labored to support themselves and their families, are told they are now entering their "golden years." If economically feasible, travel may be on the horizon. Hobbies are encouraged, as if nothing more serious can be expected. Few contemplate a second career. A variety of industries target and reap tremendous profit from this age group: long-term health insurance plans, overpriced retirement communities and assisted living facilities, memory units, senior venues where moderate exercise and crafts may be on the agenda, call centers that triage help in the event of an accident, prepaid funeral packages, ocean cruises, and more.

Becoming a grandparent or great grandparent has its own rewards. It is a beautiful thing to be able to look at our offspring and their offspring, to contemplate the many lives extending out into the world, each a human being who has that visceral connection with ourselves. I feel immensely fortunate to have four children, ten grandchildren, and three great-grandchildren, all unique people discovering their own identities and making their own ways. Many cultures honor their elders with a respect for their supposed wisdom and experience. But in too many we talk about, rather than to, them. In times of illness, I have silently raged as a doctor or other healthcare professional conversed with my wife about me in my presence.

Perhaps the most difficult change is that which occurs in those who suffer from dementia. Family members, especially those of the youngest generations, will remember those who suffer from it as they are, not entirely themselves but in a tragically diminished state. Loss of cognition is terrifying for those who experience it themselves, especially while they are still conscious of their altered capacity. A one-way street, dementia is still poorly understood, and the emphasis in management is on inability rather than on any significant gains. If we have a loving partner and can afford the help we need, we are more fortunate than those who must face this situation alone. We live much longer, on average, than previous generations, which may account for what seems like many more people experiencing a loss of their mental faculties. Or perhaps it's just that we now speak about it more openly. Other contributing factors may have to do with global warming, processed foods and generally poor diets, pollutants in the air, pandemics, and over-medication.

Old age often means being warehoused in institutions where only the most minimal needs are met. Some cultures encourage intergenerational living, and it has been shown that when very young people, the middle-aged, and the old share a living space, it can be beneficial to all involved. Young children give joy to the elderly and the elderly pass on their experience to the young. This arrangement has proven enormously beneficial to those of all ages, but it only exists in countries where a real effort is made to live the values espoused by the culture. And of course, past a certain point in a person's mental or physical decline, professional help is required.

The wealthier people are, the more easily they relegate the aged.

Memory plays a central role in all these changes and situations. Individual memories diminish with age, but people who seem to have lost all memory often recall some long-ago event in startling detail. Music is known to nudge memory in the aged. Different cultures have stories—oral or written—meant to preserve cultural memory, sharpen moral instinct, and perpetuate those values considered important to the collective and to a person's sense of self. This is why memory distortion is so insidious and its erasure so dangerous and damaging. We might all benefit if storytelling was encouraged by those of every age.

Up to now I've concentrated on individual life markers: birthdays, coming of age rituals, marriage, retirement, and so forth. But, as mentioned before, our cultures also observe collective observances, often religious in origin, such as Christmas, Yom Kippur, Ramadan, and Easter. These retain some semblance of their allegorical meanings but have been diluted by commercialism to the point where more attention is paid to modern trappings that have little to do with the traditions upon which they're based. They can be as lacking in meaningful elements as the individual celebrations often are.

Although I am not a Christian, I decorated a Christmas tree when my children were young and participated in other seasonal traditions because I wanted them to feel included in the rituals that were socially important to their friends. For decades, though, my wife and I have avoided anything smacking of Christmas. We are atheists and feel no connection to either the religious origins of the holiday or to the commodity-oriented fanfare that has consumed it.

Weathering explains the ways in which these holidays may be problematic for poor or minority populations. Other dates reference moments of conquest such as Thanksgiving and Columbus Day, or those that celebrate freedom from enslavement such as the Fourth of July, Juneteenth, Passover, Puerto Rico's *Grito de Lares*, and Mexico's *Grito de la independencia.* Because different groups of people see these holidays differently—Thanksgiving doesn't mean the same to Native Americans as it does to descendants of white Europeans—the dates may create conflict. Again, it is useful to think about how disenfranchised groups may relate or not to some of these holidays, how some of them constitute insult rather than celebration.

Beyond holidays and various markers of a life's progression, I am most concerned here with a different and rarely observed life change, the one that comes when we realize "we won't get better." These words were used recently by a friend, someone in his mid-eighties like me, to describe that moment in which he suddenly understood that the aches and pains and other physical limitations he is experiencing aren't going to go away. That no amount of exercise, physical therapy, chiropractic manipulation, dietary change, or additional medication will return him to his previous state, one in which he was accustomed to being able to easily rebound from whatever illness or accident. He is facing a different kind of future. And he is doing so largely in a social vacuum, without recognition of his changed condition by friends, colleagues, or society overall.

This is not about retirement, and it almost always postdates the onset of diminished physicality. It generally occurs in one's eighties or nineties, and although it is associated with age there is no cultural marker that recognizes it as an important milestone or embraces its challenges. On the contrary, one can expect a response of increased condescension. It may also show itself much earlier, because of illness or a serious accident. It isn't age per se but the realization that one has entered a new and extremely challenging period that defines the moment.

For those of us fortunate enough to be artists—that is, for people who create what we call art, for scientists whose work entails a constant questioning and exploration, and for other professionals whose creativity involves dealing with what we don't yet understand—the mind doesn't necessarily follow the body into incapacity. Our joints and muscles may lose their flexibility. We may be more fragile or tire more easily and require more sleep. We may be plagued with one or more of the many conditions that often accompany aging. But the way our synapses fire may involve mysterious gain as well as painful loss. The loss is obvious, the gain less so, creating a disbalance in the responses of loved ones that in turn encourages a disbalance in the person in question. This particular dichotomy has not been sufficiently studied, much less celebrated in any significant way. We don't throw a party or mark the moment. The transition doesn't have a name.

At this point, we find ourselves at an interesting juncture. A diminished capacity for recuperation signals the nearness of death, a very real sense that our time on earth is running out. This realization may bring a sudden burst of lethargy or depression. It may cause us to want to act more quickly, to try to accomplish what we feel we have yet to do before it's too late. But because we are less able, we act more slowly. Add to this situation the fact that the world has speeded up in recent decades: advances in technology and communication, condensed news cycles, noise pollution, increased violence, and the rapidity of geopolitical change all conspire to surround us with an intensity we didn't have to confront in youth or middle age. Slowing down as individuals in the whirlwind of a culture that seems to be moving at the speed of light may cause us to feel awkward, off balance, out of step with the times. Yet learning to do things more slowly can have its own rewards. An increased mindfulness may enrich both the experience and the result.

There are other tradeoffs. When I'm writing I may forget a word and must wait for it to reappear. But I am now capable of making connections and engaging in analyses I couldn't have arrived at before. Patience is required but can result in great satisfaction. Still, this life period isn't recognized except by the few cultures that really do defer to the wisdom of age, and there is no marker that celebrates its presence.

Earlier I mentioned the importance of memory. As our bodies fail us, memory takes on a special significance. But it's neither unidirectional nor fixed. Recalling easier times may be discouraging, but experiencing an awareness of the power of those times even as we are challenged to make the most of our diminished abilities can produce a depth of knowledge that is itself an asset. Memory does its own sifting, has its own rhythms and emphases. It may choose to travel unexpected byways. We need a deeper study of why and how.

In my own experience, these apparent contradictions have produced an unexpected benefit. This feels like the moment to call on my courage and speak my truth while I still can. I no longer have children to support, a job to lose, or a reputation I care about upholding. I no longer feel obliged to observe any of society's rules except those demanding honesty, kindness, and appreciation. I no longer have the need to be liked by everyone. Curiosity and conviction move front and center.

A fear of exiting life before I've completed what I feel called upon to do nudges me to direct my energy where it will enable me most expediently. Memory, the ability to make important connections, and the power to say what I believe needs to be said: these come together and urge me on. There's no name for this time of life, but all the signs of a significant milestone are there.

I am a poet. I write and then hone my poems in long sessions in which I work alone. Then comes the shared experience of workshopping with other writers and consulting with an editor to prepare a book for publication. The culmination of my poetic process comes when reading in public. Recently I had an experience that illustrates both the difficulty and the possible gifts that may come when disability imposes itself upon this activity. I had been suffering excruciating back pain that also affected my right leg and made standing unaided difficult. I was helped to the stage where a microphone hadn't been adjusted to precisely the right height and a music stand proved too rickety for me to lean on. I began to read and soon my whole body shook with the pain of trying to remain upright. I tried to keep my energy high, my voice resonant, but it became more and more difficult. Finally, wanting to be able to close on a high note, I eliminated the last poem and cut my reading short.

The audience was forgiving and supportive. They stood and applauded as I was helped off the stage. I'm not even sure how many noticed the problem. I realized too late that my dilemma had a simple solution, had I been innovative enough to think of it in time. All I needed to do was stop, briefly explain my problem, and ask for a chair from which I could have continued easily and comfortably to give my all to the full reading. Or switched positions to the edge of the stage, where I might have sat in equal comfort. Such a brief change, even without explanation or apology, would have enabled me to do my best—for myself as well as for my audience. Instead, I struggled with a situation that wasn't working and ended up feeling that I had failed. This experience led me to realize that if we pay attention to altered situations and unapologetically devise appropriate solutions, we may extend our abilities and with them our joy in making whatever contribution is ours to offer.

Some reading these musings may say this is simply about getting old, a condition that appears with differing intensity at different times in different lives and with a variety of characteristics; and that this doesn't necessarily come with the silver lining I describe. All deficit, no advantages. Perhaps. But I have witnessed this set of contradictions often enough that I believe it may be a more common occurrence than we think. It has no name, comes with no ritual marker, but has produced works throughout time that attest to its reality. Great artistic masterpieces, scientific breakthroughs, meaningful discoveries, often occur late in life when experience and the capacity for analysis combine to free our minds and passions. Might not a recognition of this time of life help encourage such works?

Does gender define important differences here? Of course it does. No matter their time of life, in almost all cultures, men are conditioned to demand that they be taken care of, their needs be met. They are encouraged to produce and given every opportunity to do so. Women's needs are neither as recognized nor as automatically considered. Our leadership is ignored or discounted. I remember the first woman national chief of police of a Central American country telling me she had to confide her ideas to male underlings and let them introduce them as their own; it was the only way she could get them instituted.

As the females of the species, we are taught from birth that our role is to make men's lives easier, provide their creature comforts, operate in the background to make them feel cared for, special. As we age, men are considered distinguished, women doddering or superfluous. As we lose our ability to do the behind-the-scenes work and keep things running smoothly, we become useless in the eyes of society.

As we age in such a culture, our lives rarely enjoy the recognition of a new threshold. We are more likely to muddle along without social markers that signal our achievements or usher in a final period. The celebrations of those who reach ninety or one hundred years tend to emphasize a life lived, not one that may still have more to offer.

What if we created a marker that truly embraces an exciting time to come rather than only what has been? We might devise a forward-looking celebration that includes the aids that encourage future work, taking into account a physical slowing-down but acknowledging ongoing possibilities: for example, a space of one's own designed with the elderly person in mind.

Everyone anticipating their final productive years or even months would have their own panorama and requirements. In fact, a time to discover what those are in each case could be built into the celebration, a preliminary period of exploration to make sure that the characteristics of the gift fit the person's needs and desires.

Some might desperately want a visit from someone important in their lives. And this need for reconnection might not always involve a beloved child or friend. I am reminded of one of my own family's patriarchs in a small South American country that suffered a cruel dictatorship in the 1970s and '80s. The man, in his nineties, had been estranged for years from his only brother. There was good reason for the estrangement. While the man in question was an old anarchist who had led a life of noble resistance in the face of his country's years beneath the fascist boot, his brother had been a high-level member of the regime, a military judge who took it upon himself to increase the sentences of many young people whose only crime had been attempting to make a more just society. Some of those young people were members of his own family. These egregious acts blurred childhood memories of earlier times, in which the brothers played together, shared boyhood secrets, their antagonistic futures unanticipated. As some in the family prepared to host a birthday party for the old anarchist, they realized he needed the almost unimaginable: a meeting with his brother. Reconciliation? Not really. Perhaps just simple contact, the chance to close a painful circle.

Family members who had been personally affected by the brother's terrorist history swallowed their rage and invited him to the party. It was a difficult hospitality. No one thought either man would betray his ideals. A simple handshake was enough. It took seconds at most but fulfilled an unspoken need. A few months later, the old anarchist died. He'd lived his final months happily, with a peace that could only have been achieved by trading politics for a human gesture that meant the world.

The foregoing is a particularly dramatic story. Most will be simpler, easier to navigate. The point is to explore the needs of the elderly who are being celebrated and to offer them something they need to move onto the next, unknown, terrain. It might be an altered routine that accounts for disability and makes room for creativity: a few packets of unusual seeds for the gardener, an evocative soundtrack for the music lover or musician, a surprise visit or ongoing accompaniment for the lonely, or an interesting recipe for the tired chef. The important thing would be to engage in deep listening, something older people don't often receive. To get to know the needs and desires of the person in question from their point of view, and then to design a celebration that opens doors rather than closes them. At this stage in life, it's important not to set goals too high. The person being honored should experience possibility, not fear of failure.

Every age has a potential for future, be that future years or days. That potential deserves a marker, a celebration of possibility that may encourage imagination and energy for the next phase and that doesn't get bogged down in cliché or commercialism. That marker can't afford to be mere ritual. A Hallmark card won't suffice. It must embrace reality as it facilitates a doing, a making, the ongoing wonder of being.

Last Words

For my grandson Sebastián, as he spars with the words of his first poems.

WORDS. Language.

As long as I can remember, I have been fascinated with the ways in which people communicate with one another. The many iterations of sound, impression, gesture, and oral memory that are passed from generation to generation. How the first peoples discovered they had the capacity to make such deliberate and discrete sounds, form words, use them to make their needs known and eventually express ideas, even abstract ones. And the great writing from every era.

The world's languages are filled with linguistic idiosyncrasies: tonalities, clicks, lisps, a tendency to the guttural or the melodic. And language isn't only manifested orally. Sign languages are like living sculpture, involving the entire body in three-dimensional expression. Braille allows the blind to read with their fingertips. And every culture also relies on non-verbal communication. The richness of how we speak to one another is a product of centuries of human brilliance and imagination.

Straightforward communication is also not enough. There is gender, inflection, emphasis, exaggeration, myth, legend, allegory, parable, metaphor, simile, rhyme, irony, humor, lies, and so many other innovative variations in the way we use words. Different cultures—different languages—privilege some of these variations over others.

Then there are the many ways in which language is transcribed to the page, or to stone, parchment, or digital platforms. The variety of scripts—from Chinese characters to Hebrew and Arabic writing to our own variation on the Roman alphabet—presents a broad range of lettering exemplified not only by many thousands of printing fonts but by as many different handwritings as there are people. The science of graphology is devoted to studying handwriting as a way of analyzing the characteristics of the person writing. It boggles my mind that by the time Chinese children graduate from high school they've memorized 4,500 characters, while we use combinations of just twenty-six letters to form all our words. And there are scripts such as Nüshu,[1] developed by and for women in a world that forced them to invent a way of communicating that was unintelligible to the patriarchy.

I delighted as each of my four children mastered the power of speech. I relished their first words, told them stories meant to increase their vocabularies. I even spoke to them in the womb. It is commonly believed that children who speak early walk later and vice versa. I don't know

1. Nüshu means "women's writing" in Chinese. It is the world's only script designed and used exclusively by women. It was developed among the rural women of the Xiao River valley in the Jiangyong country of China's Hunan province. Today it is almost extinct as few women remain who are proficient in writing and reading it.

if this is strictly true, but there is no denying the delicate dance between speech and corporal movement. One of my regrets is not having taken the time to encourage my children to learn English as well as Spanish. One of my daughters never could learn my native tongue. Another now uses it in her work. My third daughter and my son both have a working command of English because they studied disciplines that required it.

Translation has been one of my greatest joys: the ability to take a poem in Spanish and render it in English as culturally and linguistically close to the original as possible. I love the challenges of grappling with conjugation and other grammatical differences, even politics and humor. I am appreciative of inclusive expression, the increasing use of words that honor everyone, and the way modern languages have embraced egalitarian titles such as Ms. and a wider range of personal pronouns such as *them*, *they*, and *theirs*.

For many, coherent language is locked within, causing a frustration those of us who speak cannot imagine. Some are born with conditions that prevent them from ever learning oral speech; others lose the ability due to traumatic events or degenerative conditions. Recent technologies have freed that language, liberating their speakers in lifesaving ways. Stephen Hawking was an example of a brilliant mind that would eventually have been imprisoned had he not had an electronic voice synthesizer that enabled him to continue his research and communicate.

A commonly repeated nursery rhyme goes: "Sticks and stones may break my bones, but words will never hurt me." Never has an adage been less true. Words can be misleading, insulting, and injurious as well as uplifting, exhilarating, memorable. They can encourage as well as berate. A bully's taunts have too often caused suicides among vulnerable teenagers or changed the course of older lives.

Ask children who have been humiliated by their parents or others. Ask a Black man called *boy* during slavery, on through the era of Jim Crow and even today. Ask indigenous first peoples whose tribal names have been taken to designate sports teams and used in other disrespectful ways. Ask LGBTQI+ and transgender people subjected to taunts, shunning, and rejection. Ask victims of chronic pain or mental illness who are urged to "Just get over it!" Ask someone who has been told, "I no longer love you. I'm leaving you for someone else." Ask a young student who has been informed by a teacher or trusted adult that they will never amount to anything. Ask members of marginalized groups if taunts and insults never hurt. Ask any of these human beings if derogatory or ugly language doesn't diminish them, and you'll understand how powerfully words can be weapons, wounding as deeply as any other.

The idea of "last words" evokes a range of references. The phrase "having the last word" may be about winning an argument, or so exhausting your opponent that they give up. But when a person's last words are dressed in the significance of literally having been uttered on their deathbed, thus echoing in the memory of those who may have heard them or been told what they were, their impact increases.

On June 5, 1968, as Robert Kennedy lay dying on the floor of the Ambassador Hotel in Los Angeles, where he had just given a campaign speech, he raised his head slightly and asked the man cradling it, "Is everybody okay?" Then he said: "Everything's going to be okay." These phrases demonstrated his deep concern for others, a quality among many that would have made him an excellent president had he not been cut down by an assassin's bullet before he could win the office.

Robert Kennedy's last words weren't uttered in a political vacuum. Just five years earlier his brother John F. Kennedy, a sitting president, had been gunned down in Dallas, Texas.

And a few months after Robert's death, an assassin's bullet killed Dr. Martin Luther King, Jr. The United States was beginning to resemble a lawless banana republic.

John F. Kennedy's assassination was the opening crack in the modern-day law-abiding façade enjoyed by a country that prides itself on being a model of democracy. President Kennedy's wounds were so brutal that he was unable to speak; no last words of note immediately preceded his death.

In many cases less dramatic or controversial than the JFK assassination and possible coverup, the presumed murderer is caught, tried, condemned, and, if in a jurisdiction where capital punishment is legal, sentenced to death. Such people are permitted their own last words and most avail themselves of the opportunity. Some maintain their innocence. Others apologize to the victim's family. Our imperfect justice system too frequently executes the wrong person, a tragedy that has come to light in recent years as efforts such as The Innocence Project have cleared many wrongly convicted people, sometimes posthumously, at others in time to save their lives.[2]

A suicide note is the ultimate in last words, almost always inadequate for those left behind who read it hoping to gain some insight into why the person chose to take their own life. We search for reasons. We want to understand what led to such a definitive decision. We may hope to be absolved of the self-imposed guilt that we could have done something to prevent the act. We forget that the mindset of those who commit suicide rarely reflects an explanation that satisfies those who have never entertained such a notion.

2. The Innocence Project is one of several groups of lawyers and paralegals working to free the innocent, prevent wrongful convictions, and create fair, compassionate, and equitable systems of justice for everyone. Since 1989, through DNA testing, recanted testimony, and other ways of revisiting dubious convictions, 575 people have been exonerated, including 196 Innocence Project clients.

Last wills and testaments contain the final declarations of those who want to leave clear instructions for what they want done with their bodies and possessions, how they may wish specific items to be dispersed, sometimes even other sorts of final thoughts for those left behind. Most often these are simply legal documents, devoid of poetic elegance or surprise. Occasionally they include unexpected messages that can have a profound effect on family and friends.

Depending on the circumstance, last words may be random, haphazard, unintentional, or deeply meaningful. As a poet, I cherish the hope that my own last words may hold meaning. The last word in any successful creative endeavor may be life-changing.

Like most creative people, I know what I say matters. I am precise about the words I put into the world and perform them with care. Some of us may be fortunate enough to be able to ponder long and hard before we speak our last. Or our final utterings may be accidental, random, unimportant, possibly unintelligible.

A few months before beginning this essay, I suffered a small stroke. I was sitting down to lunch with my wife, opened my mouth to say something, and what came out was pure gibberish, garbled sounds neither of us could understand. I was aware that my language was failing me but couldn't do anything about it. Fortunately, within a very few minutes my speech returned to normal. I can still evoke both the frustration and the transition. The episode passed. The stroke doesn't seem to have left me with any apparent residual damage. This was an incident from which no discernible words remain, only sounds that defy understanding. Still, I often think of that attempt to speak and wonder what I was trying to say. I ended up writing a poem about the experience:

Poet Without Words

I still hear those garbled sounds,
feel my tongue like thick mud
trying to make words.

Translation didn't step in
when I opened my mouth to speak
and the words fell apart.

My ears were working and my mind
but my tongue wouldn't obey
what the brain commanded

and all I heard was thickness,
like glue, or steel wool
scouring the inside of my skull.

I cannot remember what I was trying to say
as my own words fought me and won.
Two or three minutes,

I still hold the mirror of your eyes, love,
searching for meaning in mine,
shared razor edge of fear,

enough for the word *stroke*
to take shape in my head
like a knife dipped in fire.

When the poet goes mute
the universe stops.
I don't know if she was taunting me

for those moments of terror
or whispering in my ear:
Say goodbye to tomorrow.

I can think of many utterances—poems or simple statements—by a range of writers that have meant a great deal to me. I treasure those words and often reread or repeat them to myself. They accompany me like living beings and are strong medicine in the most comprehensive sense. Today's brutally warring world provides a backdrop that may lend them greater than usual significance.

Adrienne Rich's poem "Prospective Immigrants Please Note" is one I have committed to memory. Many other poets have produced work that continues to live in me. Allen Ginsberg famously said: "First thought, best thought." He would seem to have been referring to the first words that show up in a poet's mind or on her lips, not the last. But I take his use of the word "first" not as a reference to time but to courage, energy, intuition, spontaneity.

I have often quoted the German Lutheran pastor Martin Niemöller's famous words. His warning—"First they came for the Communists and I did not speak out because I was not a Communist," along with its subsequent lines referring to socialists, trade unionists, and Jews—has been repeated ever since as the most powerful way of saying that when others are in danger and you don't stand up for them, there will be nobody left to stand up for you when you are targeted. Presumably these weren't Niemöller's last words, but they are surely his best remembered and those that have had the greatest impact.

Sometimes a person's entire life—with all its struggles and successes—is opaqued by a single statement. Such is the case when many of us think of Mexico's twenty-sixth president, Benito Juárez. I find it interesting that, as early as the mid-nineteenth century, that country elected and reelected an indigenous leader. Juárez was Zapotec, which may have taught him the importance of respectful relationships among human beings. Only a few days after Emperor Maximiliano was ousted in a coup and Juárez entered the capital city triumphant, the latter uttered his famous phrase: "El respeto al derecho ajeno es la paz"—*Respect for the rights of others is peace.* If only the world, and Mexico itself, observed that rule, we might suffer far less violence and war.

Of course, not all lasting words are spoken. Great literature is a repository for words that move, influence, and can change us.

Among literary genres, poetry is bare bones, the most concise manifestation of last words I can think of—especially if we think of last words in terms of their impact rather than timeframe. Nothing satisfies quite like the perfect poem. Words cry out for originality. Writers often say we want to create a new language, a new way of saying what needs to be said. This challenge becomes more difficult as time passes because we tend to believe everything has already been said.

As a poet, I am drawn to certain poems by poets who have gone before, especially those which in a few brief stanzas encapsulate a powerful message in a new way. The great Peruvian poet César Vallejo produced many such poems. In fact, his poetry changed the Spanish language. One poem in particular has long resonated with me. It's called, simply, "Masses" and was included in a collection Vallejo wrote after experiencing firsthand the horrors of the Spanish Civil War.[3] The poem perfectly reflects the idea that only when most or all of humanity comes together can humankind move forward. I've never found an English translation that satisfies me, so I made my own:

3. *España, aparta de mí este cáliz (Spain, Take This Cup from Me)*, 1939.

Masses

The battle was over,
the combatant dead, and a man approached
pleading: "Don't die, I love you so!"
But the corpse, aye, it kept on dying.

Two came and they too implored:
"Don't leave us! Courage! Return to life!"
But the corpse, aye, it kept on dying.

Twenty, a hundred, a thousand, five hundred thousand
arrived, crying out: "So much love powerless against death!"
But the corpse, aye, it kept on dying.

Millions surrounded him
with a single plea: "Don't leave us, brother!"
But the corpse, aye, it kept on dying.

Then all the earth's inhabitants
surrounded him; the corpse looked at them in sorrow,
was moved, slowly rose
to embrace the first person; began to walk...

Sometimes the words great poets or writers leave us appear contradictory and force us to dig deep to see if we agree or not. I feel this way about African American poet Audre Lorde's famous statement about the master's tools. In an influential essay, Lorde wrote: "For the master's tools will never dismantle the master's house. They may allow us temporarily to beat him at his own game, but they will never enable us to bring about genuine change."

At first, the meaning of Lorde's statement seemed clear to me, and I accepted it at face value. I love her poetry, her mind, and wouldn't have questioned any of her affirmations. But my own subsequent life experience taught me that sometimes we must develop new tools to fight a powerful enemy, while at others his own tools can be used against him very effectively. We can see evidence of this in all the struggles of the last half of the twentieth century and first decades of the twenty-first. I'm grateful for those words of Lorde's not because I believe them to be true in all cases, but because they make me think. And they make me realize it's important to question absolute prescriptions even when they are written or uttered by those we deeply admire.

A writer who, more than any other, can literally be said to have left us with her last words was Meridel LeSueur. Meridel was born with the century in 1900. She grew up in a socialist family in the Midwest, rode freight trains in the 1930s selling little poetry chapbooks for a penny, and eventually became an important writer. Her work reflected the previously ignored realities of women and working people. Her novel *The Girl*, written in 1939, failed to convince a publisher for decades because books with strong female protagonists were all but impossible to place. It finally saw the light forty years later when a small independent press called West End issued a first edition. Later, feminist publishers appeared who retrieved other important works by LeSueur.

Meridel lived a long and active life. We were friends, and she gave me some personal words unusual in their perspective that helped me understand who I am. When I returned to the United States and was faced with deportation because of the content of several of my books, many people I knew commiserated and offered support. Meridel was supportive but didn't commiserate. She wrote me a note in which she told me how proud of me she was that my work had warranted the government's negative response: "It would have been awful if they'd have admitted you without a fight," she said.

But these weren't the last words of Meridel's to which I referred earlier. Her final few years were spent in a nursing home. There she unionized the staff and kept on writing. Her daughter Rachel Tilsen visited her almost daily. One morning Rachel arrived to find her mother, aged ninety-six, dead on the bed, papers scribbled with her barely intelligible writing scattered about her.

As she was dying, Meridel had been writing about her experience of that transition, the complex feelings it entailed. Feelings so powerful they demanded her attention even as her great vitality waned. Rachel collected the pages and gave herself to the task of deciphering and recreating what has come to be known as Meridel's final poem. Titled "This with my last breath," it begins:

> This is like adolescence – all your body is
> changing ... the glands ... the center glandular
> shift ... fast changes.
> Substance tempo another kind of sleep ... my
>   reality seems different ... I am a stranger to
>   myself ...

If ever last words conveyed the culmination of life experience, including the physical reality of dying, these are surely extraordinary among them.

I want to acknowledge my gratitude to Gregory Randall, Barbara Byers, Greg Smith, and V. B. Price, who read or listened to many of these essays at earlier stages and provided important input. I also want to thank Zach Hively for going over the finished book with a fine-tooth comb and making it so much better. I feel fortunate to be able to count on the support of these friends.

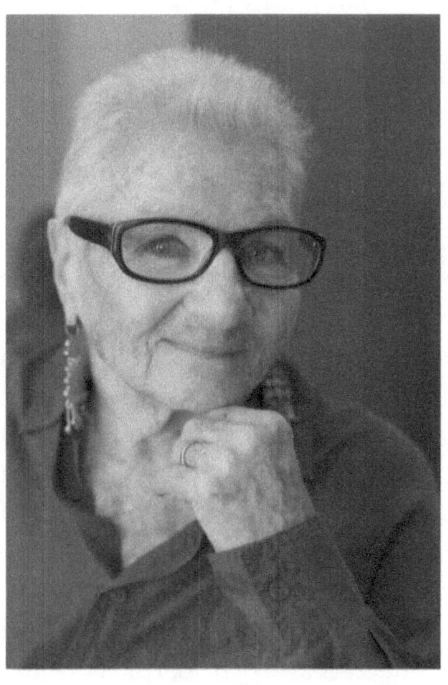

Margaret Randall (b. New York, 1936) is a poet, essayist, oral historian, translator, photographer, and social activist. She lived in Latin America for twenty-three years (in Mexico, Cuba, and Nicaragua). From 1962 to 1969, she and Mexican poet Sergio Mondragón co-edited *El Corno Emplumado / The Plumed Horn*, a bilingual literary quarterly that published more than seven hundred writers and visual artists from thirty-five countries: some of the best new work of the sixties. When she came home in 1984, the government ordered her deported because it found some of her writing to be "against the good order and happiness of the United States." With the support of many writers and others, she won her case, and her citizenship was restored in 1989.

Randall's most recent poetry books include *Against Atrocity* and *Out of Violence into Poetry* from Wings Press, and *Home*, *Vertigo of Risk*, and *Stormclouds Like Unkept Promises* from Casa Urraca Press. *Time's Language II: Selected Poems 2019-2023* follows *Time's Language: Selected Poems 1959–2018*, both from Wings Press, as compendiums of her best poems. Nonfiction titles include *Che on My Mind* (a feminist poet's reminiscence of Che Guevara, published by Duke University Press), *Thinking about Thinking* (Casa Urraca Press), *Artists in My Life*, and *Luck* (New Village Press). In 2020, Duke published her memoir, *I Never Left Home: Poet, Feminist, Revolutionary*. Many of these titles have appeared in Spanish translation from Siglo XXI, Alforja, Ediciones de Medianoche, and Heredad in Mexico; Casa de las Américas, Ediciones Matanzas, and Vigía in Cuba; Abisinia and Tinta Limón in Argentina; Rumbo in Uruguay; and small independent publishers in Cuba, Nicaragua, Brazil, Ecuador, Peru, Colombia, Venezuela, Spain, Holland, Japan, Turkey, and India.

Randall also translates from Spanish. She has translated poetry collections by Roberto Fernández Retamar, Roque Dalton, Otto-René Castillo, Carlos María Gutiérrez, Daisy Zamora, Kelly Martínez, Israel Domínguez, Alfredo Zaldívar, Laura Ruíz, Chely Lima, Rita Valdivia, Reynaldo García Blanco, Yanira Marimón, and Gaudencio Rodríguez Santana, among others; novels by Freddy Prestol Castillo, Juan Antonio Hernández, and Tomás Modesto Galán; memoirs by Gregory Randall, Lurgio Gavilán Sánchez, and Stefano Varese; and anthologies of Cuban poetry and short stories, Ecuadorean poetry, US poets for Mexico, and Beat poets in Spanish. She has read her own work and delivered keynote addresses in hundreds of venues throughout the United States, in Latin America, and occasionally in other countries.

Two of Randall's photographs are in the Capitol Art Collection in Santa Fe. In 1960, she was a recipient of a Carnegie Fund for Writers Aid Grant and a grant from the American Academy of Arts and Letters revolving fund for writers in need. In 1989, she was a co-winner of the Mencken Award, and in 1990 she received a Lillian Hellman and

Dashiell Hammett grant for writers victimized by political repression. The Barbara Deming Money for Women Award was given to her in 1997, and in 2004 she received the PEN New Mexico Dorothy Doyle Lifetime Achievement Award for Writing and Human Rights Activism. Randall received the 2017 Medalla al Mérito Literario from Literatura en el Bravo, Ciudad Juárez, Mexico. In 2018 she was awarded the Poet of Two Hemispheres prize by Poesía en Paralelo Cero in Quito, Ecuador. She received an honorary doctorate of letters from the University of New Mexico in 2019. In 2020 she received the George Garrett Award from the Association of Writers & Writing Programs (AWP) and the Paulo Freire Award from Chapman University. In 2022 she received the City of Albuquerque's Creative Bravo Award. Randall lives in Albuquerque with her partner (now wife) of more than thirty-seven years, the painter Barbara Byers, and travels extensively to read, lecture, and teach.

Casa Urraca Press publishes creative works by authors we believe in. New Mexico and the US Southwest are rich in creative and literary talent, and the rest of the world deserves to experience our perspectives. So we champion books that belong in the conversation—books with the power, compassion, and variety to bring very different people closer together.

We are proudly centered in the high desert somewhere near Abiquiú, New Mexico. Visit us at casaurracapress.com to browse our books and to register for workshops with our authors.

www.ingramcontent.com/pod-product-compliance
Lightning Source LLC
Chambersburg PA
CBHW030933060726
47591CB00005B/1775
* 9 7 8 1 9 5 6 3 7 5 3 4 3 *